Half Past Autumn

For Momma and Poppa

I stay drenched in the showers of their love.

Half Past Autumn

A RETROSPECTIVE

Gordon Parks

ESSAY BY PHILIP BROOKMAN

A BULFINCH PRESS BOOK

LITTLE, BROWN AND COMPANY

Boston New York Toronto London

IN ASSOCIATION WITH THE CORCORAN GALLERY OF ART

CREDITS

Half Past Autumn: The Art of Gordon Parks is organized by the Corcoran Gallery of Art, Washington, D.C. This exhibition and related programs are made possible by Ford Motor Company and Time Warner Inc. Additional support is provided by the Glen Eagles Foundation, Cone-Laumont Editions, Ltd., Laumont Labs, and Time Life Photo Laboratories.

Ford TIME WARNER

ACKNOWLEDGMENTS

THIS BOOK ACCOMPANIES the exhibition *Half Past Autumn: The Art of Gordon Parks,* organized by the Corcoran Gallery of Art, Washington, D.C. This project, which celebrates and documents all of Gordon Parks's many accomplishments, has been made possible through the encouraging assistance and contributions of many people. We are particularly indebted to Mabel H. Cabot at Ford Motor Company and Toni G. Fay at Time Warner Inc., whose generous support has made this exhibition and its related programs a reality. The contributions of co-curator and colleague Deborah Willis have been invaluable. We also extend our appreciation to Zachary Morfogen of Morfogen Associates, whose perceptive understanding of the complex administration of this undertaking has kept it on track. For their enormous contributions, special thanks must go to publisher Carol Judy Leslie of Bulfinch Press, Little, Brown and Company, and to editor Terry Hackford, who have intelligently crafted this book. The production of the exhibition has been a multilayered task. At the Corcoran Gallery of Art we are beholden to David C. Levy, Jack Cowart, Annie Davis, Paul Roth, Susan Badder, John Chappell, Joy Hallinan, Cindy Rom, Kirsten Verdi, Jan Rothschild, Jan McNamara, Ken Ashton, Lisa Ratkus, Kat Yakaitis, Elizabeth Parr, Steve Brown, Katy Ahmed, and interns Mary Jo Aagerstoun, George Kimmerling, Shannon Thomas, and Jessica Udvardy. For their attentive assistance with production of exhibition and publication materials, we are indebted to John Cone and Andre Ribuoli of Cone-Laumont Editions, Ltd., New York, Philippe Laumont and Stuart Ward of Laumont Labs, New York, and Heike Hinsch, Tom Hubbard, and El Kazan of Time Life Photo Laboratories, New York. Thanks also must go to Bernard Reilly, Maricia Battle, Beverly Brannon, and Verna Curtis at the Library of Congress, and Peggy Parsons and Alan Shestack at the National Gallery of Art. Finally, we would like to thank the artist Gordon Parks and his assistant Johanna Fiore for their unyielding, ongoing, and invaluable support of this project.

Philip Brookman, Curator of Photography and Media Arts
Corcoran Gallery of Art, Washington, D.C.

EXHIBITION TOUR

Corcoran Gallery of Art Washington, D.C.
September 10, 1997 – January 11, 1998

Minnesota Museum of American Art St. Paul, Minnesota
February 14 – May 14, 1998

Museum of the City of New York New York, New York
July 1 – November 1, 1998

Detroit Institute of Arts Detroit, Michigan
February 7 – April 25, 1999

Norton Museum of Art West Palm Beach, Florida
October – December 1999

Michael C. Carlos Museum, Emory University Atlanta, Georgia
February 5 – April 9, 2000

New Orleans Museum of Art New Orleans, Louisiana
June 3 – August 27, 2000

California African American Museum Los Angeles, California
October 13 – December 30, 2000

Cincinnati Art Museum Cincinnati, Ohio
February – April 2001

Chicago Historical Society Chicago, Illinois
October – December 2001

FIRST EDITION

The text in this book is based in part on previously published versions of Gordon Parks's autobiography, recast in new form and from the author's current perspective for this volume. A complete list of the author's books can be found in the bibliography on page 354. Some of the photographs in this book have also been previously published in books by Gordon Parks.

Library of Congress Cataloging-in-Publication Data
Parks, Gordon, 1912 –
Half past autumn: a retrospective / Gordon Parks; essay by Philip Brookman.
p. cm.
Accompanies the exhibition organized and held at the Corcoran Gallery of Art, Washington, D.C., Sept. 10, 1997 – Jan. 11, 1998, and nine other museums, Feb. 14, 1998 – Dec. 2001. Includes bibliographical references and index.
ISBN 0-8212-2298-8 (hc), 0-8212-2503-0 (pb)
1. Parks, Gordon, 1912 – — Exhibitions. 2. Afro-American photographers — Biography — Exhibitions.
3. Photography, Artistic — Exhibitions. I. Brookman, Philip. II. Corcoran Gallery of Art. III. Title.
TR140.P35P35 1997
770′.92 — dc21 97-19797
[b]

Designed by Eric Baker Design Associates, Inc.

Bulfinch Press is an imprint and trademark of Little, Brown and Company (Inc.)
Published simultaneously in Canada by Little, Brown & Company (Canada) Limited

PRINTED IN ITALY

Contents

Kansas:
The Early Years

Boy with June Bug, 1963

Author riding horse on Kansas prairie
Photograph by David Parks

PARTING

Two roads passed my father's house
They went everywhere, with tolls
Unfixed on unmarked distances
Paved with roses and thorns.
He said a few things
When I was packed to go;
The feel of your feet
Will reconcile the differences
Of which road you take.
There will be signposts
along the way
Giving out devious directions.
It's your right to question them.
But don't ignore them.
Each one is meant for something.

You will find that summer grass
underfoot will be kinder
To your touch than autumnal weeds
Yet, during winter storms,
It will be the taller stalks
Leaning above the snow
That will catch your eye.

And you will learn
that
All the same things
Are really not the same,
that
You must select your friends
With the same care I gave
To choosing your mother, or
Maybe the wood to build fences.
Avoid things that die too easily
And get your own soul ready
to die well.
Don't get gray by yourself,
And don't be surprised
When as you grow older
You begin to pray more
And worry less.
Remember most that everything
I have told you might very well
amount to everything
Or
Perhaps nothing. But be most thankful, son,
If in autumn you can still manage a smile.

Prairie Land, 1949

Prologue

THE YOUNGEST OF FIFTEEN CHILDREN, I was born in the small prairie town of Fort Scott, Kansas. There my mother and father, Sarah and Jackson, helped me endure the tempest of racial bigotry. Death took my mother when I was only fifteen. Most of my brothers and sisters had already gone off on their own. Worn thin, seemingly helpless without his wife, Poppa honored Momma's final request and sent me north to live with one of my older sisters, Maggie Lee. His parting words are still with me: "Just follow your Momma's teachings and you'll be all right." Then somewhat hesitantly he touched my shoulder, sighed, and went off to feed his hogs. Before the flowers on her grave wilted I was on a train to St. Paul, Minnesota.

It was a frightening leap to a big metropolis that would wash over me like a cold sea. Before long, my disgruntled brother-in-law threw me out. It was night. The temperature was thirty degrees below zero. That night I sought shelter at a pool hall until it closed, then rode streetcars between St. Paul and Minneapolis until dawn to escape the cold. Frightened, alone, I was far from those I loved. And even in this north country, bigotry was still hanging around. In the years that immediately followed I barely survived by playing the piano in a brothel and washing dishes at a dingy restaurant. But an urge to create had taken hold, though the little art I had been exposed to was that found in "funny papers." The closest thing to classical music I'd heard was the humming of june bugs in Poppa's cornfield. Poetry came with greeting cards — hardly the verse of a Pablo Neruda or a Henry Wadsworth Longfellow.

Sarah Parks, author's mother

Preoccupied with survival, I looked back to the heaven and hell of Kansas and asked some questions. My memories gave me some straight talk. "The important thing," they said, "is not so much what you suffered — or didn't suffer — but how you put that learning to use." Looking back meant recalling childhood friends who perished by guns or knives. Hostility wasn't the answer. Fierce emotions had to be salved through what Momma had called good common sense. Then came hills to climb and roads to walk that, at times, seemed to carry me backward. Five books I've written are thick with those memories — all with leftover smells of the long journey. Finally, after a long search for weapons to fight off the oppressions of my adolescence, I found two powerful ones — the camera and the pen.

In Kansas, always my touchstone, there had been infinitely beautiful things to celebrate — golden twilights, dawns, rivers aglow in sunlight, moons climbing over Poppa's barns, orange autumns, trees bending under storms and silent snow. But marring that beauty was the graveyard where, even in death, whites lay rigidly apart from blacks. Twenty-odd years had passed when, with these things lying in my memory, I returned to Kansas and went by horseback to lock them firmly with my camera. Spring was wrapped around the prairies. Nothing much had changed — certainly not the graveyard.

Andrew Jackson Parks, author's father

Since then I have roamed distant corridors of the planet where nature's wonders never end; where, in some place or another, humanity reveres or defiles them. Tyrants, dictators, dethroned kings, beggars, queens, harlots, priests, the uplifting and the despoilers — all stared into my camera with eyes that were unveiled. The camera revealed them as they were — human beings imprisoned inside themselves.

Now, inspiration arrives suddenly at times — shaped by words, music, art, and the mysteries of life. A musical theme vibrates my sleep. I get up, go to the piano, and jot it down. A blustery sky, a crescent moon, or the blazing sun can hurry me to poetry or the camera. When the doors of promise open, the trick is to quickly walk through them. Things inside me are still sprouting upward; still working overtime. Racism is still around, but I'm not about to let it destroy me. Too much grave digging is going on, and firing anger at each other only keeps up the digging. If we would only remember the needs of our past, perhaps we could anticipate those of our future.

These images and words are a gathering of individuals, events, places, conflicts, and dilemmas that confronted me as I shifted from course to course in pursuit of survival. Some, star-colored, others, painted with rage, fall like rain in my memory. They all simmer down to what I remember, forgot, and what at last I know.

GORDON PARKS

FOLLOWING Lane in Fort Scott, 1963

ABOVE Frisco Railway Station, Fort Scott, 1949
OPPOSITE Mrs. Jefferson, Fort Scott, 1949

Shoes, Fort Scott, 1949

Death Room, Fort Scott, 1949

OPPOSITE LEFT Mrs. Mullens, Fort Scott, 1949
OPPOSITE RIGHT Uncle James Parks, Fort Scott, 1949
ABOVE Pool Hall, Fort Scott, 1949

MOTHER
POLLY ANN
JOHN STINGLEY
May 9, 1802
DIED
JOHN STINGLE
BORN
DIED
FEB 23, 187

OPPOSITE Gravestones, 1949
BELOW Benedictine Monastery, 1955

OPPOSITE Outhouse, 1949
ABOVE Chicken Hawk, 1949

KANSAS LAND

I would miss this Kansas land.
Wide prairie filled with green and cornstalk;
the flowering apple,
Tall elms and oaks beside glinting streams,
Rivers rolling quiet in long sleepy summer days
For fishing, for swimming, for catching crawdad
beneath the rock.
Cloud tufts billowing across the round blue sky.
Butterflies to chase through grass high as the chin.
June bugs, swallowtails, red robin and bobolink,
Nights filled with soft laughter, fireflies and restless stars,
The winding sound of crickets rubbing dampness from wings.
Silver September rain, orange-red-brown Octobers
and white Decembers with hungry smells
of hams and pork butts curing in the smokehouse.
Yes, all this I would miss —
along with the fear, hatred and violence
We blacks had suffered upon this beautiful land.

Frisco Railway Station, Fort Scott, 1949

Photography: The Beginning

THE FIRST FROZEN WINTERS IN MINNESOTA had offered me a number of roads that could have led to a bad end. Without doubt it was the earlier teachings of right and wrong that kept me straight. When I reached twenty, the harshness of my existence was tempered by the experience of falling in love for the first time. Sally Alvis, a beautiful young lady with an engaging smile, became my target after I met her on a blind date. From then on I aimed flocks of arrows toward her heart. They struck, and, following a frenzied courtship that went on for nearly twelve months, we took our marriage vows. A year later Gordon Jr. was born. Three more years passed before our daughter, Toni, arrived.

Still suffering cruelties of my past, I wanted a voice to help me escape it. In 1938 a camera I bought for $7.50 would become that voice. The decision struck after I watched Norman Alley's remarkable newsreel footage of the strafing of the American gunboat *Panay* by Japanese planes. Until then I had survived in a number of ways — playing the piano in a brothel, washing dishes in a restaurant, and busing dishes in a hotel. At the time I was working as a waiter on the North Coast Limited, a transcontinental train running between St. Paul, Chicago, and Seattle. In a magazine left on the train I found pictures taken by photographers of the FSA, or Farm Security Administration, a government agency set up by President Roosevelt to aid submarginal farmers. The subjects: dispossessed migrant workers. Beaten by storms, dust, and floods, they roamed the nation's highways in battered jalopies and wagons. Others pushed their young in baby buggies and carts. Homes were shanties patched together with scrap woods.

The photographers' names stuck in my mind: Dorothea Lange, Arthur Rothstein, Russell Lee, Carl Mydans, Walker Evans, Ben Shahn, John Vachon, Jack Delano, Marion Post Wolcott, and John Collier. All worked under Roy Stryker at the FSA. The stark, tragic images urged me on — to John Steinbeck's book *In Dubious Battle,* to Erskine Caldwell and Margaret Bourke-White's book *You Have Seen Their Faces,* and to what became my Bible, *12 Million Black Voices* — a powerful statement against bigotry, with text by Richard Wright and photographs from the FSA files. I bought that Voightlander Brilliant at a Seattle pawnshop; it wasn't much of a camera, but, for only $7.50, I had purchased a weapon I hoped to use against a warped past and an uncertain future.

Sally Alvis Parks, author's first wife, 1934

Meanwhile Poppa had moved to St. Paul, and I photographed him shortly before he died. I still remember his sitting on a log with his eyes peering into the lens, asking, "Son, what's that gadget you've got there?"

"A camera, Poppa. It's called a Voightlander Brilliant."

"Funny name, I'd say." As always, he was right.

I AM OFTEN ASKED why I didn't allow anger and bigotry to maim me. The answer lies in the goodness of people who, regardless of their color, reached out to me when I needed help. Without them, the most inconsequential hills would have been impossible to climb.

Vivid in my memory stands Madeline Murphy, a woman of Irish descent. In 1940, married, the father of two small children, laid off from my job, hungry, and desperate, I entered her exclusive women's store in St. Paul, sought out her husband, and asked to photograph their fashions. He was showing me out the door when she asked, "Frank, what does the young man want?"

"He wants to photograph fashions."

"Well, how do you know he can't?"

Frank groaned as she asked me to sit down in one of the store's princely chairs.

"Can you photograph fashions?" she asked.

"Yes, ma'am," I lied.

"Do you have any examples of your work?"

"No ma'am, I'm sorry."

After a few moments of thought she stunned me: "I'm going to give you a chance. Be here at six-thirty tomorrow evening after we close. How many models do you want?"

"Ah, ah — three."

"How many outfits?"

"Ah — six."

"What kind?"

"Well — formal things."

Frank was still groaning when I left.

The following evening I arrived with lights and a highly sophisticated camera — one I had never used before. (Both were borrowed from a friend, Harvey Goldstein.) The models and clothes were all there, and, nervously, I went to work. Madeline was impressed. Frank was impressed. Even I was impressed — until later that night when I developed the film. With the exception of one exposure, the entire batch was double-exposed. The hostile camera had failed me.

Owing Madeline honesty, I put my thoughts in order. Two mornings later, when she and Frank arrived at the store, a large print of the one good exposure stood in front of the store on an easel. Madeline's first look brought joy to her face. "Its beautiful! Come in and show us the others!"

I gave her the truth. Frowning, she asked, "Would all of the others have been as good as this one?"

"Oh," I said, "that's probably the worst."

She gave me another chance. No double exposures. Marva Louis, the wife of Joe Louis, the world-champion boxer, visited the store and observed the results that had been displayed on the counters and in the windows. Impressed, she invited me into a much larger arena for fashion photography — Chicago. To bolster her invitation she also promised to help me find work. I packed to leave with a question gnawing in my mind, and one afternoon I went to Madeline for the answer. "Why, when Frank was kicking me out the door, did you come to my rescue?"

She thought for a few moments. "I don't really know. Perhaps I was just mad as hell at Frank about something." I knew better. It was her goodness that pulled me back through that door.

Tough, challenging, Chicago would give me some bad moments — moments when I would come close to giving up. But Madeline's voice kept calling from blind corners, "Don't stop now." A few of Chicago's fashionable ladies sat before my camera. But I began focusing on the city's south side, where poverty ensnared the huge black population. Within a year the body of work I accumulated there brought me the first Julius Rosenwald Fellowship awarded to a photographer. Then came the miracle: Roy Stryker took me on to serve out my fellowship at the Farm Security Administration in Washington, D.C. I had

Fashion, Frank Murphy's, 1940

Roy Emerson Stryker, Washington, D.C., 1942

fallen into a well of luck.

I arrived in Washington in 1942 to work alongside the very best documentary photographers — a goal that had kept haunting me after I saw their pictures of those impoverished migrant workers. Four years had gone by since then. I knew very little about Washington, other than that beneath its gleaming monuments and gravestones lay men with famous names in American history. Sensing my ignorance, Stryker sent me out to get acquainted with the rituals of the nation's capital. I went with enthusiasm. The sky was without clouds; the entire universe seemed to greet me with promise.

But soon my contentment began crumbling. In this radiant, historic place, racism was rampant. White restaurants shooed me to the back door. White theaters refused me. The tone of white clerks at Julius Garfinckel's department store riled me. Clothing I had hoped to buy there went unbought. They didn't have my size — no matter what I wanted. Washington had turned ugly. I hurried back to Stryker. My face told him everything. Pulling on his coat to leave, he asked, "Well, how did it go?"

Self-portrait, 1945

"Mississippi couldn't have been much worse. What's to do about it?" I asked.

"It's bad — very bad. That's why I was hesitant about taking you on here. You're not going to have an easy time of it. You'll have to prove yourself to them with superior work." He paused for a moment. "Obviously you ran into some bigots out there this afternoon. Well, it's not enough to take one person's picture and label it *Bigot*. You have to get at the source of their bigotry. And that's not easy. The camera becomes a powerful weapon when put to good use. Talk to other black people who have spent their lives here. Their experiences might help you to become more aware of racial problems in this city. Go through these picture files. The photographers who produced them are saying a lot about what's happening in this country today. That's what you must do eventually."

I followed his advice, spending many hours with the picture files. Then the day came when I met Ella Watson, a black charwoman who was mopping the floor at the FSA. I watched her for a few moments, then eased into conversation with her. Within fifteen minutes she had taken me through her lifetime of bigotry and despair. "Would you let me photograph you?" I asked. "I don't mind," she answered.

So it happened that, in one of the government's most sacred strongholds, I set up my camera for my first professional photograph. On the wall was a huge American flag hanging from the ceiling to the floor. I asked her to stand before it, placed the mop in one hand, a broom in the other, then instructed her to look into the lens.

After placing her photograph on Stryker's desk two days later, I nervously awaited the verdict. He looked at it and shook his head. "Well, you're catching on, but that picture could get us all fired." Washington now had a black charwoman, standing erectly with mop and broom before the American flag. Her title: *American Gothic*.

American Gothic, 1942

Ella Watson and Her Grandchildren, 1942

Children with Doll, 1942

Church, Washington, D.C., 1942

ABOVE Pastor Ledbetter, Chicago, 1953
RIGHT Sunday Morning, Washington, D.C., 1942

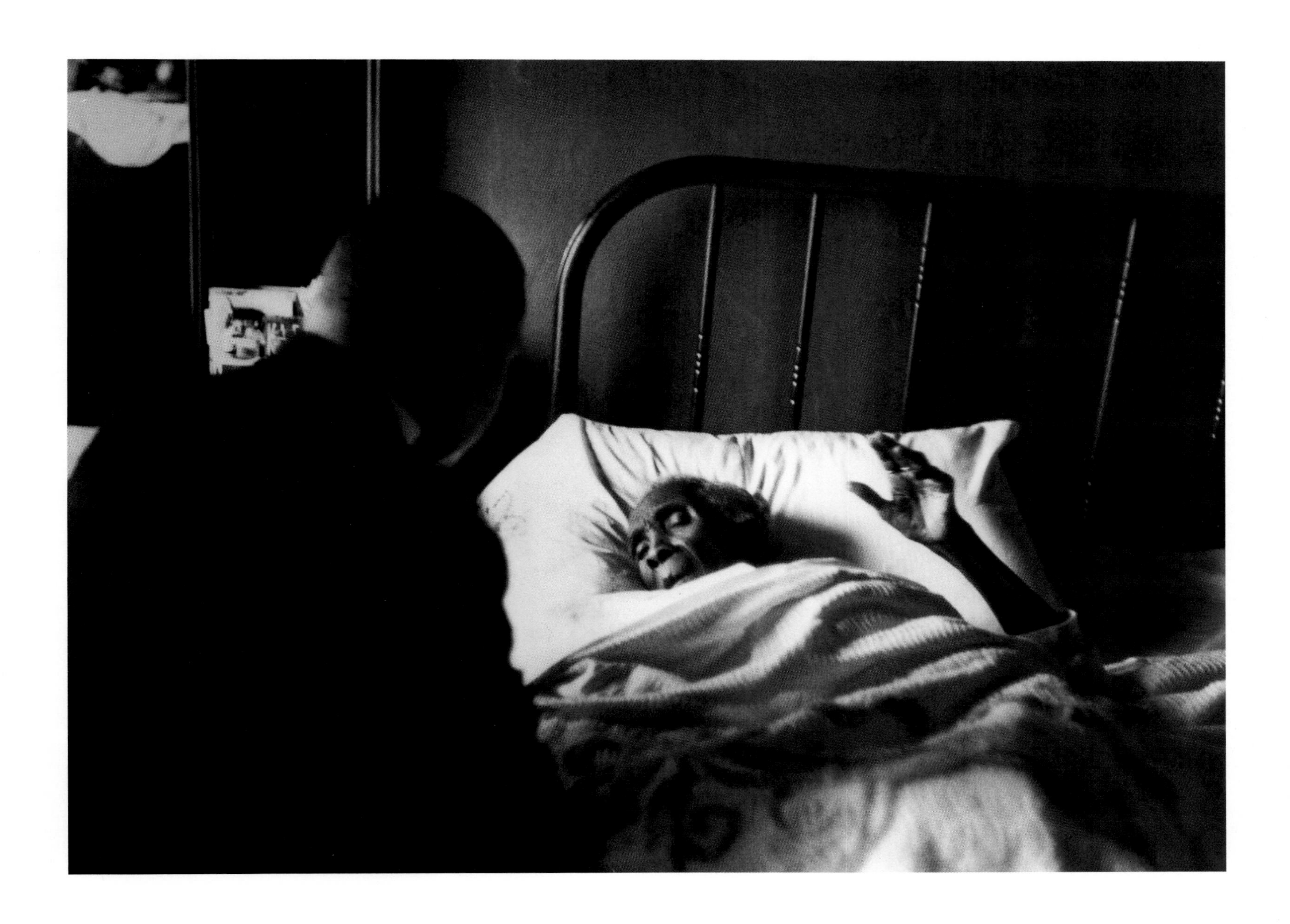

OPPOSITE Babe Ruth's Funeral, New York, 1948
ABOVE Woman Dying, 1953

FOLLOWING
LEFT Tenement House, Ansonia, Connecticut, 1949
RIGHT Man with Straw Hat, Washington, D.C., 1942

Harlem Newsboy, Washington, D.C., 1943

Children at an Interracial Camp, Haverstraw, New York, 1943

Amish Children, 1945

New England Countryside, 1949

ABOVE Ferry Commuters, Staten Island, New York, 1944
OPPOSITE Grease Plant Worker, 1945

ABOVE New England Family, 1943
OPPOSITE Mother and Child, Blind River, Ontario, 1955

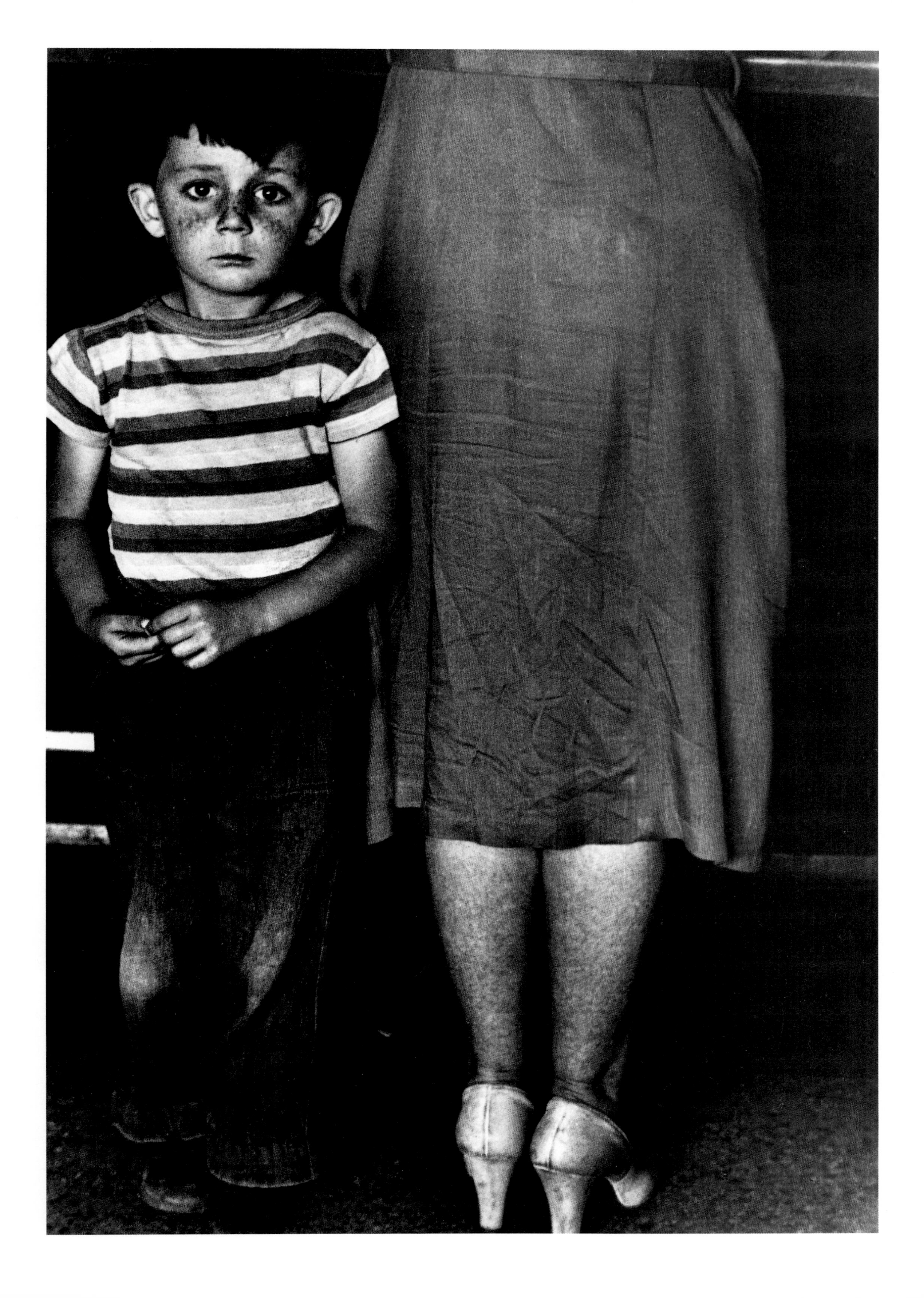

OPPOSITE Car Loaded with Furniture on Highway, 1945
ABOVE Drugstore Cowboys, Blind River, Ontario, 1955

ABOVE Farmer, Springfield, Connecticut, 1945
OPPOSITE Abandoned House in Augusta, Maine, 1944

ABOVE Storm, Atlantic Ocean, 1942
OPPOSITE Hercules Brown, Somerville, Maine, 1944

4 for 10
UNCONDITIONALLY
CEILING PRICE
10
INVOICE
Serve Anytime!
REFRESHING·
DELICIOUS·
Enjoyed by the whole Family
ONE BOTTLE
MAKES 5 GALLONS
EX-LAX
EX-LAX
EX-LAX
SAXON
SAXON
LUX
Stickney and Poor's
Medicated
25¢
10¢
30¢
15¢
40¢
50¢
60¢
5¢
10¢

Harlem: Riot

RICHARD WRIGHT, THE AUTHOR, was on a list of black Americans whom I wanted to photograph during my apprenticeship as a Rosenwald Fellow in Washington. It was a hot August afternoon in 1943 when I reached New York to keep an appointment with him. As I drove up Harlem's Lenox Avenue, people were huddled on stoops and leaning out of windows, trying to get relief from the heat. I had parked my car when suddenly I heard shouting. Then all around me people were running, smashing windows and looting. Police cars were careening in from both ends of the block. Cops spilled into the streets with drawn guns and billy clubs. An elderly white clerk was grabbing at two black teenagers who were making off with a radio and electric toaster. A fist smashed into his jaw and he collapsed to the sidewalk. A cop went after the two boys as they ran between the cars. Two women were hurrying past, one with an armful of clothing, the other with two bottles of whiskey. I was dead center in a Harlem riot. A cop ran toward me brandishing a pistol. "Drop that bag!"

His pistol was still pointed at me when I took out my credentials and showed them to him. "I work for the government!"

He scanned them quickly. "Okay, git the hell outta here!" He then went after two men making off with a piece of furniture. Glancing back I saw a huge woman swinging at another cop with an umbrella. Drenched with blood, an elderly black man sat on a stoop, moaning. Some teenagers were trying to overturn a patrol car. A tenement building owned by a white real estate company was ablaze. A fireman was rescuing an elderly woman by ladder from the third story. Anger had taken over Harlem. I fled across Seventh Avenue.

Wright shook his head sadly the following morning when I told him about my experience. "It was a mad scene out there. You could have been killed." The fame that *Native Son* had brought seemed not to have touched him. After I photographed him we talked about the black man's problems in America. I had brought along a copy of *12 Million Black Voices,* for which he had supplied the text. He inscribed it, "To one who moves with the new tide." So often I had read the inspiring passage in that book: "We are with the new tide. We stand at the crossroads. We watch each new procession. The hot wires carry urgent appeals. Print compels us. Voices are speaking. Men are moving! And we shall be with them."

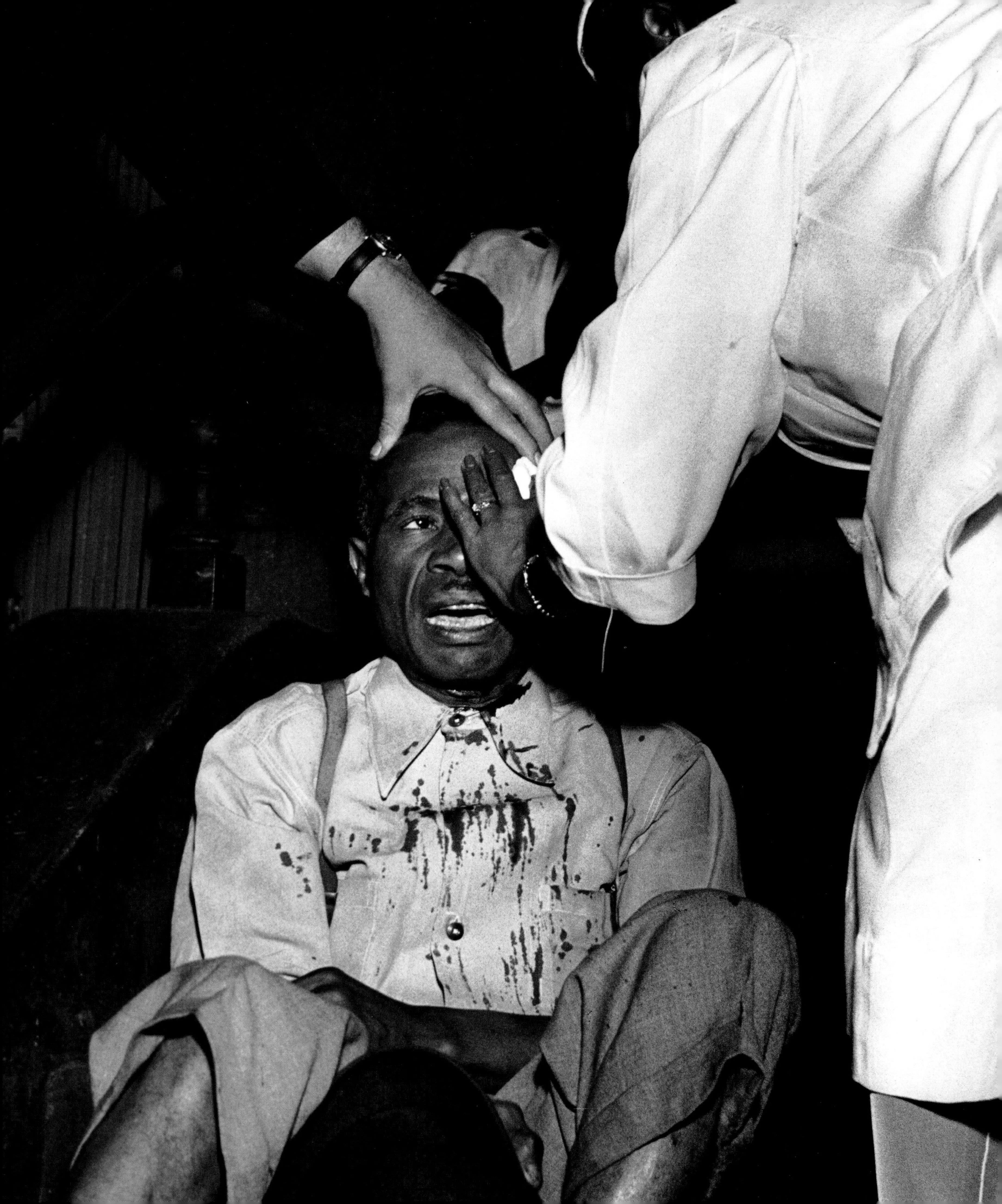

DRINK

As I left Harlem later, things had calmed down, but a menacing voice was still feeding the disquiet on Lenox Avenue. "Big Roz" was on his soapbox: "I'm tellin' you like it is! White cops all around us with death in their guns! Harlem's just another Mississippi! I'm here to bury these gun-totin' white devils no no I ain't scared of none of 'em their day is comin' to an end and I'm pushin' that day along run 'em out of Harlem our children are bein' shot down with guns bought with our tax money stop prayin' to that white God for help he ain't carin' nothin' about you so quit runnin' to his dog-ass church and fallin' on your knees All the fuss was about a depression and we've been depressed for three hundred years those white bandits suck our blood like leeches and our so-called black leaders are out in whitey's kitchen beggin' and Mister Whitey gives them a crust of mangey bread to keep the other negroes up here in Spooksville quiet you and me hafta solve our own problems cause our leaders pardon my expression ain't shit the only way to fight whitey is with guns and money oh yes we hafta have money whitey hands you the bible and keeps the money for hisself fight fire with fire nobody gonna hurt you now it's too many of us here so brothers and sisters put a nickle dime quarter or dollar in this can thank you brother thank you sister come closer don't leave I've got plenty more to say . . ."

Roz's accusations were hardly secrets. Harlem was thick with the proof of them — on the streets, in the dirty alleys and crumbling tenements. After listening for several minutes I walked on, with his voice still running through my body.

BLACK PICTURE OF CHRIST
By SHERMAN SCHOFIELD FURR

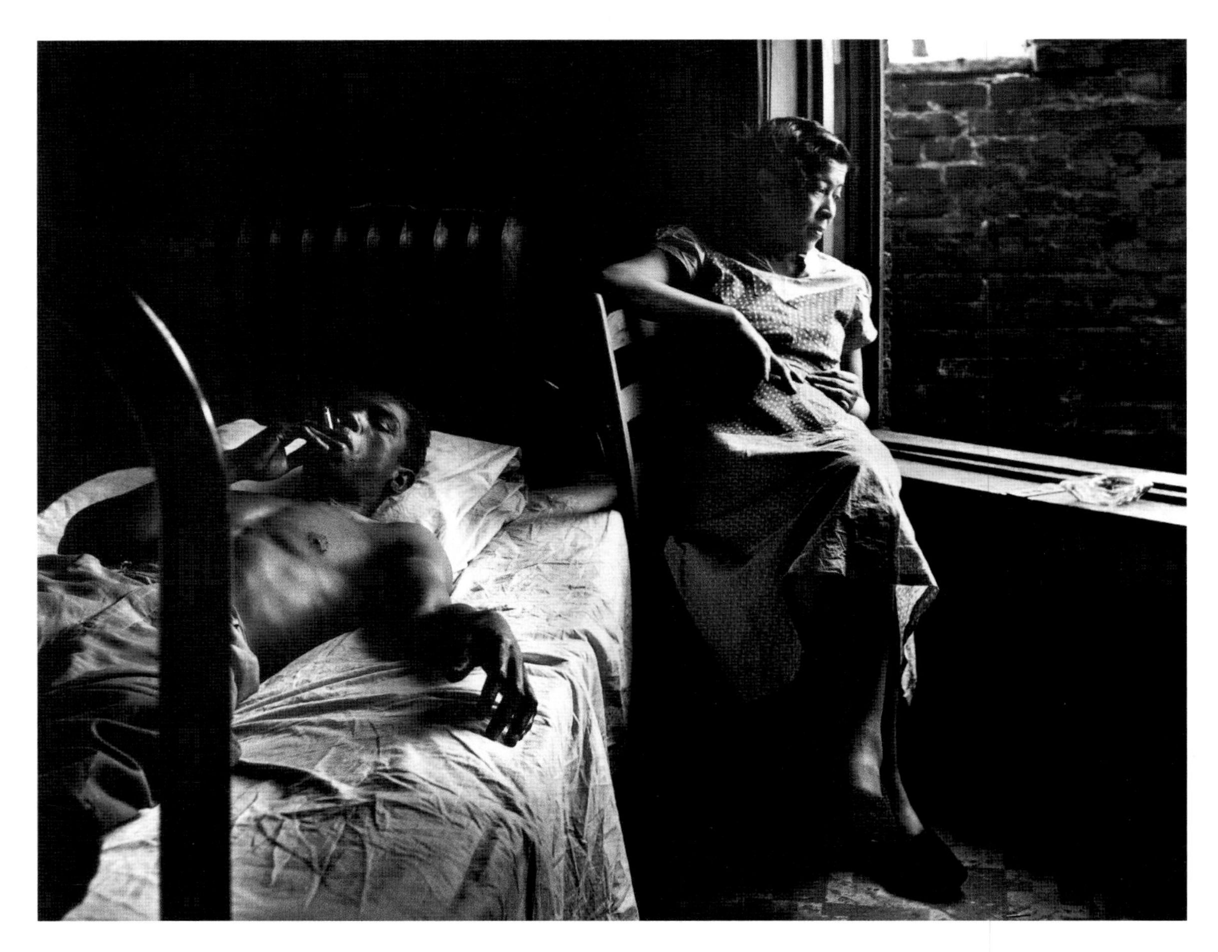

Coca-Cola
7up
YOU LIKE IT IT LIKES YOU

Black Fighter Pilots: Racism

SOUTHERN SENATORS AND CONGRESSMEN had gnawed the Farm Security Administration to pieces by 1943. Its picture files, crammed with America's poor and dispossessed, practically amounted to the government's indictment of itself. Overnight the agency was abruptly abolished and absorbed into the Office of War Information (OWI). Stryker moved to OWI and took certain photographers with him. I was one of them, and, for me, the transition was so smooth it seemed all but unnoticeable.

America was in the second year of World War II. Unrest was building in black military quarters. William Hastie, a black aide to Secretary of War Stimson, had resigned because of discriminatory practices against Negroes in the air force. The black 99th Pursuit Squadron, after a bitter struggle against racism, had finally been formed, trained, and sent overseas. Before long it had distinguished itself under the leadership of Colonel Benjamin O. Davis Jr. Now, the 332nd Fighter Group, the first of its kind, was in training under his command at Selfridge Field near Detroit, Michigan. Within a week I was assigned to it as a war correspondent. I was to cover it in training, then record it in combat overseas. Suddenly I was caught up in the excitement of covering a war. Not until later would I realize that nothing justified the burden I was placing upon my pregnant wife, Sally. Gordon Jr. and our daughter, Toni, were already on her hands when I left for Selfridge Field. Now she was about to give birth to David.

The hot air smelled of petrol when I reached the base. A squadron of P-40 Thunderbolts was roaring overhead, and black pilots were flying them. On the days to follow I was up at six, then, after a quick breakfast, hurrying to the flight line with camera and a notebook. Minutes later the planes were airborne with young black fighter pilots — getting ready for a fight with Adolf Hitler's *Luftwaffe*.

Bad weather had set in and all flights were grounded. Five of us were playing poker when the voice came over the intercom: "Redbird to tower. Redbird to tower. I'm floundering. Bring me in. Over." It was Jimmy Higgins.

"This is the tower. We're socked in here, Redbird. Try for Oscoda. Over."

"Fuel's gone. I've got to come in. Give me a bearing. Over."

"You're too high and too far north, Redbird. Circle sixty degrees left. Let down slowly. Over."

A few minutes later an ominous whining pierced the wet morning air, growing louder, nearer. Jimmy's Thunderbolt was out of petrol and spinning downward. Bill Walker dropped his cards. "Bail out, man," he said softly. Then came the crash. A short distance away Jimmy Higgins lay crumpled inside it.

When Judy Edwards's plane spun out up near Oscoda, Michigan, a week later, his body had to be taken to Detroit — because there were no facilities for handling Negro dead in Oscoda. Lieutenant Tony Weaver, who accompanied the unembalmed remains, remarked, "That three-hundred-mile journey amounted to a long, sad trip. I feel shame for having to wear this uniform."

OPERATIONS
PILOT
MISSION
REMARKS

Author in war correspondent's uniform
Photograph by U.S. Air Force

Disaster remained wed to the days of training, but such losses were par for the course. Captain George Knox powered our Thunderbolt up to fifteen thousand feet and leveled off. Above and to our right, Bill Walker was leading a trainee through the turns. Knox shook his head. "That's a hairy job with new men!" We climbed higher, keeping the two planes in sight. Suddenly the horrible thing was happening. The trainee's propeller was chewing up Bill's tail. We watched as the two broken planes plummeted toward earth. Knox banked sharply and passed over them as they struck the ground. Then he called the tower. "This is Bluebird. Bill's gone. I'm coming in." I, like all of his fellow pilots, had grown fond of Bill Walker. Now there was no morning as sorrowful in the world.

During mid-December all furloughs were canceled. Training was finished; we would be going overseas. Traveling orders came a week before Christmas — and for me, some disturbing words from Colonel Davis. "Parks, we're about to pull out, and your papers are not in order."

"What's wrong with them, sir?"

"You'll have to take that up with Washington. I'd advise your flying there immediately. Otherwise we'll be en route to our port of embarkation before you could get an answer."

I reached Washington on a weekend. Elmer Davis, the OWI chief, was away, but the next morning Ted Poston, a writer in the press section, took me aside. "My friend," he said, "there's some politicians who resist giving the Negro pilots publicity. That's your real problem."

That afternoon, at 14th Street and Independence Avenue, Captain Lee Rayford, Lieutenant Walter Lawson, and I waited for the bus that would take us to the Pentagon. Both were pilots from the 99th Pursuit Squadron who had just returned to America after flying against Hitler's *Luftwaffe*. Captain Rayford, holder of the Purple Heart, the Distinguished Flying Cross, the croix de guerre, the Air Medal, and the Yugoslav Red Star, had been shot down over Austria. Both men, having flown their required missions, could have remained Stateside as instructors. Instead they had volunteered to return to the war zone.

We had taken our seats behind the bus driver when he snarled, "If you fellas wanta ride into Virginyuh, you gotta go back to the rear!" We ignored him. He stood up, a scrawny, disheveled man with stained teeth and a hawk nose. "You heard what I said. This bus ain't goin' nowhere till you move to the back, where you belong."

We continued to ignore him. "Okay, I'm callin' the MPs and havin' you put off!"

"Start calling," Rayford replied. Two white captains and a major were seated across the aisle, stirring uncomfortably. Several other whites sat in the near-empty bus. An elderly black woman stood up, and her look demanded that we stay there. The driver stood glowering at us. One of the white captains leaned over and spoke softly. "Fellows, we know how you feel about this, but the major has an urgent appointment at the Pentagon. He would appreciate it if you would move to the back so we can be on our way."

The old woman was still standing up, grasping the seat ahead of her. Borrowing the captain's icy politeness, I addressed the major. "These men are fighter pilots just back from fighting Hitler. I'm from the Office of War Information. Would you like to order these two highly decorated officers to the rear? Otherwise, we have no intention of moving."

After a moment of thought the major motioned to the driver. "Let's go, man. Can't you tell when you're licked?" The driver hesitated for a moment, then plopped into the seat and slammed in the gears. We lurched off toward Virginia.

"Hallelujah!" The old woman's voice rang with triumph. Rayford and Lawson smiled. To them, it amounted to a small victory. To the old woman, it was a mighty conquest.

"Thank God we don't have to sit in the back of those P-38s," Rayford quipped as we parted at the Pentagon. "See you on the other side."

The sergeant in charge of overseas traffic looked at my papers. "Far as I can see, they're in order."

"Then why was I sent back here?"

"Beats me."

"Thanks. Now where can I rejoin the 332nd Fighter Group?"

"That's classified information. I'll give you directions as far as Newport News, Virginia. You'll have to play it by ear from there. I'm not allowed to give the exact location." He handed me a map and penciled in a wide circle. "It's inside there somewhere."

At a bus station in Newport News I rode a hunch and wrote out a government order for a ticket to a destination where I felt the pilots would be. The agent examined it, then looked at me suspiciously. "Where'd you git this?"

"It's a government-issue slip for travel."

"I know what it is, but I ain't never heard of no Negro writing one out."

"I'm with OWI, and I'm my own issuing officer."

"No ticket unless you've got cash."

A younger man stepped to his side. "Are you with the black Fighter Group?" he asked.

"I'm surely not with a white one."

"You don't need a ticket. Wait. I'll make a telephone call." He came back shortly after. "It's arranged. Someone will pick you up in front of the building within the next half hour." Twenty minutes later an army command car arrived with two WACs. My spirits rose as we sped toward Camp Patrick Henry.

The pilots gave me a rousing welcome. I gave them the two bottles of scotch and three cartons of cigarettes I'd brought. Aside from women these were the things they craved most. Money seemed useless now, and they gambled it away with abandon. But there had been trouble on the base. A black ground crewman had been beaten up by white paratroopers two days before. The black pilots were fighting segregation at the movie house and on chow lines. The mood was bad.

New orders came during the week. We would sail two days earlier than planned. There would be far fewer problems at sea than on this troubled base. Colonel Davis sent for me at midday. He spoke calmly but ice was in his voice. "A call from Washington. Your papers are not in order. You won't be able to travel with us. I'm sorry."

"They didn't find anything wrong with my papers at the Pentagon. Can't you protest in some way?"

"There's absolutely nothing I can do. Orders from there cannot be rescinded." I had lost. As I turned and started out he called to me. "You are aware that strict secrecy is to be kept about our travel plans."

"I understand. Don't worry."

I couldn't bring myself to say good-bye to the pilots again. I packed quickly, slipped through a rear door, and boarded an army chopper for Washington. From there I would fly to New York.

We were circling near Washington. Far below I could see the landing field, lying like small strips of cardboard under wispy patches of clouds. Farther out in the distance the monuments shone milk-white in the winter sunlight. The water in the mall sparkled like an oblong jewel between the sculptured trees. The Capitol stood quiet and strong on one end; the Lincoln Memorial sat on the high quarter of the opposite slope. A beautiful sight wed to human ugliness. Somewhere down there were doors still closed to black people. I thought back to the fighter pilots. They would soon be at sea, sailing toward war and death, despite their differences with this land they were about to defend. And reluctantly I was returning to the heart of those differences.

We were landing. The intolerance of Washington came rushing in as the chopper landed. There would be an hour's wait here before I took off again. I just wanted to get out quickly. I strode into the air terminal, tired, hungry, and irritated. Every white face looked to belong to the Klan. My entire body was rebelling against the frustrations of the past week. I slammed down my gear and sat down by a white man. His creased neck, thin lips, and beady eyes were a reminder of that bigoted bus driver. One wrong word and I was set to pounce on him. Turning, he looked me over and spoke casually. "'Morning, soldier. Good day for flying." He pulled out a pack of cigarettes, offered me one, and lit it.

With some difficulty I came to terms with myself— blew out the smoke and confusion with one breath. "Yep, a very good day for flying."

A friendly word from a stranger had lifted me temporarily from the darkness. Two hours later I was landing in New York, en route to its mean streets. As my taxi reached the high point of the bridge, a stretch of dreary Harlem rooftops widened on the horizon. I had no idea what the next day would bring, but instinct told me that I wouldn't perish. I was ready to fight bigotry or poverty. The significant thing, yet again, was the choice of weapons with which to fight. At Lenox Avenue trash was swirling up from the gutters. But within the icy wind Momma's words were echoing from the past: "Work hard and have faith in yourself."

Captain George Knox

ABOVE Bill Walker
OPPOSITE P-40 in Line for Takeoff
FOLLOWING 332nd Fighter Group in Flight

E20

Fashion

WHILE I CONTINUED to do some assignments for OWI, in 1944 I took a cheap room at Harlem's YMCA and began looking for steady work. Sally and our children had gone back to live with her parents in Minneapolis. Counting on her forbearance, I began the search.

Sometime later, Alexey Brodovitch at *Harper's Bazaar* studied my fashion pictures for several minutes. "They're marvelous," he finally said, "but this is a Hearst organization, and it forbids our hiring Negroes. I'm sorry." The past had come back again. I thanked him and left. That same day I spoke with Roy Stryker, who suggested that I go see the renowned photographer Edward Steichen. I found him at his Fifth Avenue office wolfing down a corned-beef sandwich, then told him about my experience at *Harper's Bazaar.*

"Brodovitch, the son-of-a-bitch," was his reply. He then scribbled a name on a piece of paper and handed it to me. "Go see this man at *Vogue* and see what he has to say."

That afternoon I watched as Alexander Liberman examined my work, and I sensed another refusal in the air. At last he laid my photographs on his desk and said simply, "We're going to give you a chance." Words that were sweet music to my ears.

Tina Fredericks, a senior editor at Condé Nast, was given the job of acquainting me with the various offices. Gracious, friendly, and extremely knowledgeable about fashion, she gently steered me through my first assignments. Six months had passed when, with a mellowing smile, she gave me some radiant news. "Alex has selected you to photograph a collection of the season's finest evening gowns. It's a major assignment. Congratulations." I was somewhat shocked, but the joy that overtook me was inexhaustible. "Your photographs are beautiful." This remark from Alexander Liberman after the story appeared was what I had been hoping for. The eight pages of color that appeared were, to me, the apogee of the opportunity given to me. Quietly I rejoiced at those *Vogue* pages, and for the next five years my work would continue to appear in them. It was a good time, a joyous passage blossoming with beautiful clothes and vibrantly lovely models of that era. And with an undying love for both, I pursued them in Paris and other worldly bastions of haute couture for decades to come.

Gang Warfare: Harlem

PHOTOGRAPHING FASHIONS was rewarding but, for me, somewhat rarefied. Documentary urgings were still gnawing at me, still waiting for fulfillment. In 1948, after several good years at *Vogue,* I took courage and walked through *Life* magazine's door one afternoon — without an appointment — to ask for a job. Wilson Hicks, the magazine's tough picture editor, looked up at me and frowned. "How'd you get in here?"

"Just walked in."

"Then you can damn well turn around and walk out."

I laid a stack of photographs on his desk. "Fine, but can't you take a quick look at my work first? You might like it."

He observed me for a moment, then glanced at my pictures — and kept on looking. Then gruffly he mumbled a question that caught me off-guard. "Got something in mind that you'd like to do?"

Not expecting things to go that far, I quickly concocted an answer. "Gang wars up in Harlem — and fashions." He thought it over for a few moments, then called in Sally Kirkland, *Life*'s fashion editor, and John Dillie, a feature story editor. Both viewed my work, and their smiles said that they were impressed. Sally needed a fashion photographer to cover the upcoming Paris collections. Dillie needed someone to photograph an essay on crime. Hicks, after a few minutes of thought, decided to give me a try. Suddenly for me, two extremely diverse worlds were about to converge — one of crime, the other of high fashion.

I began work on the crime story with a frustrating search for a way to gain access to a gang. Finally I stumbled upon Red Jackson, a sixteen-year-old Harlem gang leader. He was at the 125th Street police precinct where, to my astonishment, he was cursing out a desk sergeant. Jimmy Morrow, a detective friend, explained: "He leads the Midtowners, the toughest gang up here. We hoped he could cool things off by pulling his gang back, and we promised him protection, but one of his gang was cut up and dumped into the Harlem River the other night. That's why he's in here raising hell."

I followed Red into the street. After some nudging, he allowed me to give him a ride to 116th Street. When I explained what I wanted, he asked a rather sensible question. "Why in hell would I want a *Life* photographer following me around? Ain't I got trouble enough?"

"Maybe I can be of more help to you than the cops were. Furthermore, you'll have my car to ride around in." After we reached his destination he got out and gave my Buick a long glance. "I'll talk with my war lords tonight. Meet me here tomorrow afternoon." My car had done its job. Two days later I was driving Midtowners around Harlem.

A month later I was given a fashion assignment. Then I rejoined the Midtowners. Red's perilous existence was a far cry from the perfumed houses of high fashion. Such a double-faced reality posed the kind of readjustment that was hard to come by — especially after a Midtowner was badly knifed during a rumble.

Despite their show of bravado the gang members seemed to sense that death was lurking around every corner. Their families also lived in constant fear. With their sons caught

OPPOSITE Red Jackson
FOLLOWING Harlem Rooftops

OPPOSITE Gang Member with Brick
BELOW Neighborhood of Gang Warfare

up in beatings, knifings, and sporadic gunfire, they had good reason. Hostility claimed the lives of four boys during that brutal period — two from Red's gang. Before long I came to like Red. At times I suggested that there was a better way of life for him. He would listen in silence, seeming to agree. But the violent trappings of gangdom would stay on, mobilizing his circumstances against such advice. The Midtowners would go on paying with their lives.

When, three months later, the essay was being readied for publication, I objected strenuously to the cover that had been chosen. A smoking gun in Red's hand could have sent him to prison. The trust that had grown between us was at stake. I reclaimed the negative then cut it to pieces.

"Mr. Parks!" Forty years had passed when the gruff voice stopped me in New York's Pennsylvania railway station. A thick-set, neatly dressed middle-aged man came toward me, smiling. "Remember me?"

I observed him closely. The crooked jaw, the freckles, the reddish graying hair suddenly came together. I grabbed his hand. "Red Jackson!" He went on for an hour rehashing those fearful days of his youth. Fortunately, talk of the Mafia's rubbing him out had been just a rumor. He had just turned fifty-six. Just before departing he jolted me with a suggestion. "You know, you and me could go back up to Harlem together and save some of those kids up there. I'm always asking myself about how I got into so much trouble."

"That's fine, Red. And I hope we can get together." We exchanged a high five then he disappeared into the crowd. Later I received a letter from Red and the promise of a phone call. For nine years I've awaited that call. I often wonder if he is still around — still asking his past a lot of unanswerable questions.

OPPOSITE Fight
ABOVE Daylight Rumble

Night Rumble

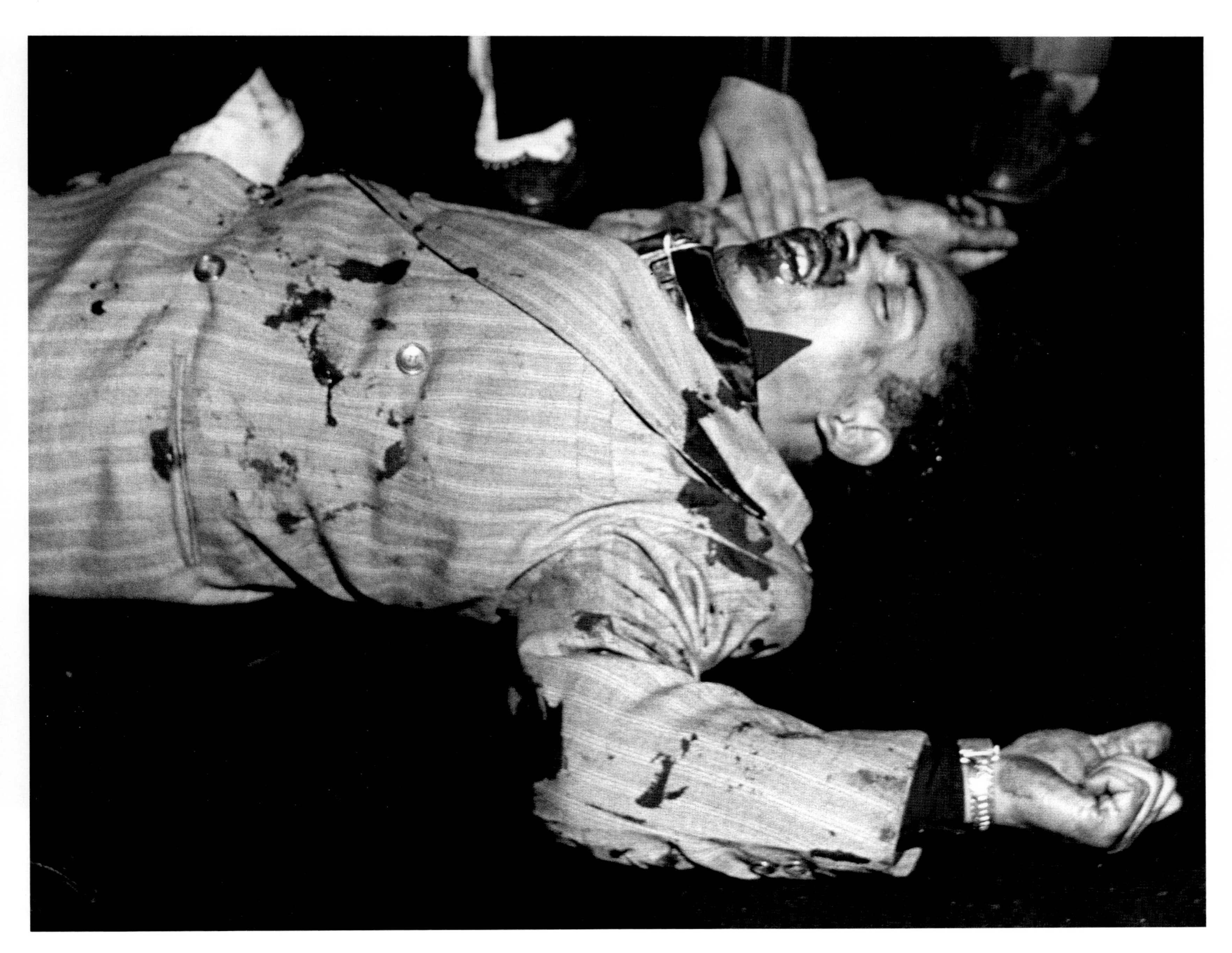

Gang Victim

ABOVE Harlem Neighborhood

OPPOSITE Red Jackson and Herbie Levy Study Wounds on Face of Slain Gang Member Maurice Gaines

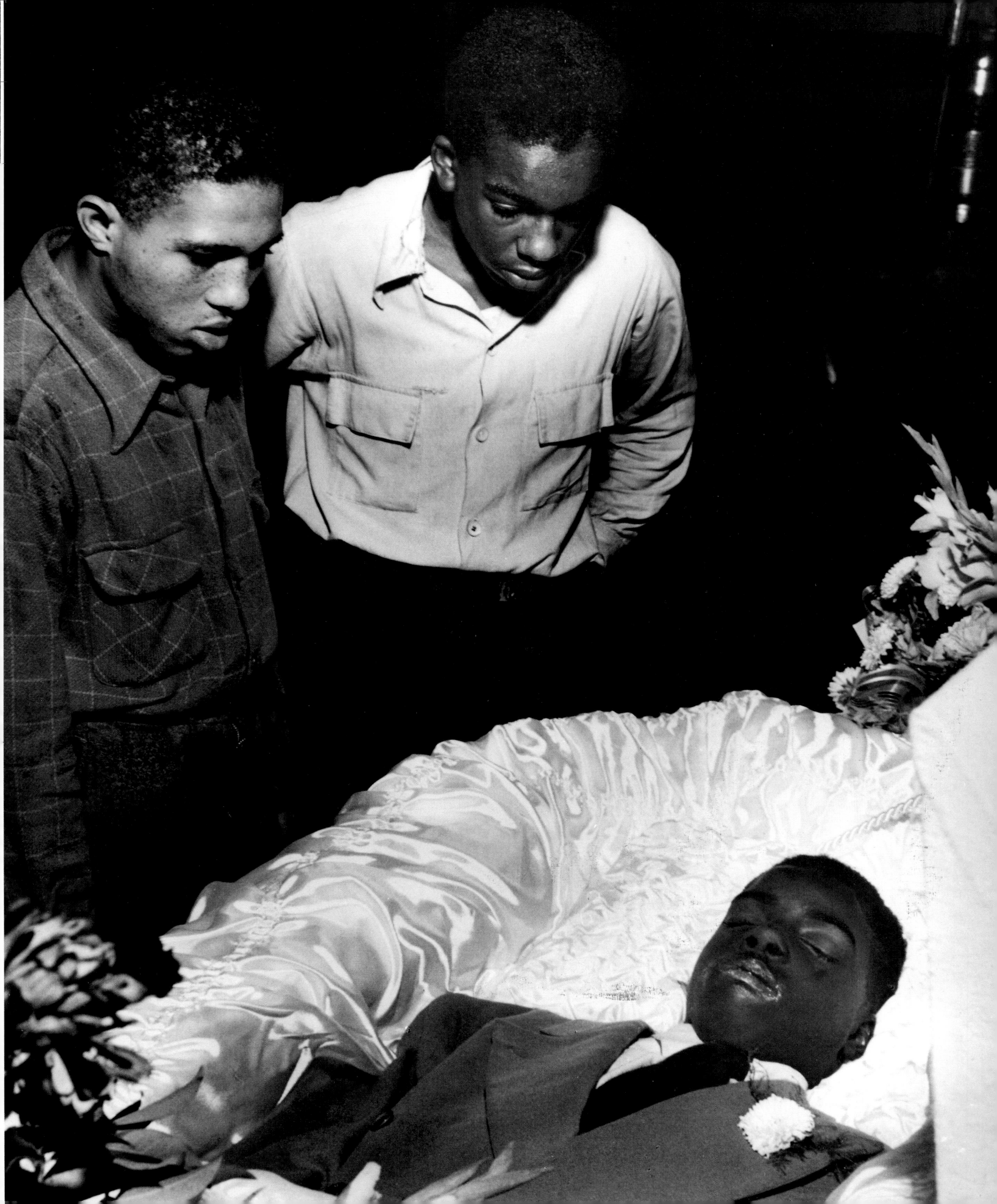

Europe and the Early Years at *Life*

RESPONSE TO THE HARLEM GANG ESSAY brought recognition. Letters poured in from *Life*'s readers — some sympathetic, others vitriolic. Henry Luce, the magazine's founder, sent a short congratulatory note. Then Wilson Hicks called early one morning with some news that took care of all my dreams: "We have decided to send you to Paris to cover the French collections." I sat silent for several moments — stunned. Paris, a city I had never dreamed of entering, was suddenly beckoning to me.

After taking leave of my wife and children, then living in White Plains, New York, I sailed for France on the *Queen Mary* with *Life*'s fashion editor, Sally Kirkland. A cablegram arrived from Wilson Hicks while we were aboard the *Queen Mary*. He was offering me a job on staff — at a salary that sent my thoughts skyward. When Sally read the message, she smiled, then gave me some sound advice. "Accept his offer — but on your own terms." I promised to follow her instructions. When we arrived in Paris, another cable awaited me: OKAY — YOU'RE ON STAFF WITH A THIRD MORE THAN PREVIOUS OFFER. CONGRATULATIONS. I cabled back how happy and honored I was.

For me, Paris was a golden time. The melodious names of the great fashion houses bounced around in my head — Chanel, Dior, Molyneux, Schiaparelli, Fath, Balenciaga, and others I found difficult to pronounce. All the beauteous mannequins were there — Dorian Leigh, Bettina, Janine Klein, Jackie Stoloff, Suzy Parker, Carmen, Dovima, and others who graced the pages of prestigious fashion magazines. My thoughts, a long way from the cornfields of Kansas, were soon drowning in the worlds of Degas, Matisse, and Renoir. When, after two weeks, the assignment ended, the magical dream died, and my film was put on a plane en route to New York.

My work in Paris brought me some congratulatory letters from *Life*'s editors, Henry Luce, its founder, and from readers across the nation. But one from St. Paul, Minnesota, was the most deeply appreciated: "Dear Gordon. Saw your beautiful Paris fashions. Your talent is still alive and growing. I'm proud of you. Madeline Murphy."

Madeline Murphy and author at the Minnesota Club, where author was once a busboy, 1970
Photograph by St. Paul Pioneer Press

Place de la Concorde, Paris, 1950

PRECEDING PAGES Paris Fashions, 1950
ABOVE Spanish Fashion, 1950

I WAS PACKING FOR MY RETURN FROM PARIS when another cable from Wilson Hicks arrived, instructing me to proceed to the island of Stromboli to cover the Bergman-Rossellini affair. Maria Sermolino, from the Rome bureau, would accompany me.

The two harried lovers were ensconced on a volcanic island in the Tyrrhenian Sea. It was a bad time for them. Most of the world was looking upon Ingrid with shame. Roberto, with great difficulty, was directing a motion picture in which she was starring. Newsmen and photographers besieged them; helicopters with more cameramen hovered above. Exasperated, he had ordered all of them off the island. I never knew why *Life* was invited, but obviously they felt the magazine would handle the situation with discretion.

Ingrid was smiling and waving as our boat slowly edged toward shore. But Roberto was spewing wrath at a reporter in an outgoing boat. "Go! If you return you will die at my hand! You are a fascist ingrate and a liar!"

"Addio, tyrant, pig, wife stealer!" came the reply. Enraged, Roberto splashed through the water in pursuit of the boat. By then it was well out to sea.

Bad weather and trouble had set in. The film wasn't going well. What's more, it was reported that Dr. Lindstrom, the jilted husband, was sailing toward Stromboli for a showdown. Despite her distress, Ingrid appeared unruffled amid the confusion. Maria Sermolino had plenty of news to report. Her problem was getting it off the island without Roberto's censorship. He lorded over the cable office and the people who staffed it. Messages could be sent by the boat that came from the mainland three times a week, but Sermolino strongly suspected that the ship's officers were also under Roberto's control. Her suspicions were confirmed when a message to the Rome bureau about Dr. Lindstrom's pending arrival failed to reach its destination. It had been returned to Roberto, who had it placed on Sermolino's bed. After that the two seldom spoke to each other.

I admired Ingrid as a person and as an actress, and, despite Roberto's Gestapo-like tactics, I grew to like him. In his less harried hours, his charm and gentleness shone through. He treated her with tenderness and concern, and one could sense her warm feelings for him. Unfortunately, he was under pressure most of the time, filming less and less as costs steadily mounted.

During Ingrid's free time we roamed Stromboli by foot, shooting pictures of her for the coverage. She was gracious, kind, and easy to work with. Before long a sense of trust grew between us, one I honored. We were walking the beach when she suddenly stopped. Looking out to sea, she said, "Roberto's losing touch with the film. The wonderful locations where you have photographed me seem to have escaped his eye. Would you consider staying on to assist him?"

Surely I was surprised. "That's a very flattering offer, but Roberto would never agree to it."

"I'd like to try." Later that evening she did try. Angrily he refused. The matter was dropped.

Ingrid Bergman at Stromboli, 1949

What every magazine longed for was a photograph of that unguarded moment when the two lovers might surrender to an embrace. I accidentally wandered into that moment one evening after everyone had left the set except the two of them. Innocently, they stood holding on to one another in the center of a large room, tired, drained from their ordeal. I was about to raise my camera when her trust in me struck; the moment was undeserving of betrayal. I put the camera in my pocket and slipped out, allowing the moment to slip away.

On Sunday morning Ingrid knocked at my door. "Roberto and I are going for a boat ride and a walk along the shore. Would you like to join us?"

"I would love to."

"Then bring your camera. We would like some nice pictures together."

Soft rain was falling as we started off. After a short boat ride they began their walk. And, as unobtrusively as possible, I recorded their peaceful journey along the beach of black volcanic sand. That sought-after moment I had allowed to escape was generously rewarding me.

Maria Sermolino and I left the island at dawn a week later. The waves, I remember, were angry as we boarded our ship. Maria went to her quarters, but I remained on deck, my camera trained on smoke curling over the volcano of Stromboli. From the distance its cone seemed to be slowly sinking into the sea. Soon, the two lovers would awake to yet another day of trouble, heartache, and uncertainty. My thoughts drifted toward Ingrid's most crucial ordeal. In changing her life to pursue happiness, she was caught up in the despair of deserting one child while another one, fathered by Roberto, grew inside her. But nothing stopped the love flowing between them. It would stay until death turned up for both of them.

Ingrid Bergman and Roberto Rossellini on Island of Stromboli, 1949

TIME BECAME THICK WITH MEMORIES when *Life* sent me back to Fort Scott, Kansas, where I had attended a small segregated school. My assignment was to find the eleven members of my junior high school graduation class and see how they had fared since my departure twenty-three years before. Their names were easy to recall: Emmaline Smalley, Emma Jane Wells, Margaret Tyson, Mazel Morgan, Luella Russell, Pauline Terry, Donald Beatty, Ira MacNear, Earl Collins, Fred Wells, and Peter Thompson.

Luella and Fred were still there. Donald had moved to Cleveland. Mazel was in Chicago; Emmaline was in San Diego. Emma Jane and Peter (now husband and wife) were in Kansas City; Margaret in Chicago; Pauline in Detroit; Ira in Phoenix, and Earl in St. Louis. After weeks of searching I found all of them — except Emmaline. Her mind, I was told, had gone, and she was being kept behind locked doors in San Diego. The others seemed to be doing rather well, except for Mazel. I found her bruised from a beating, delivered by the drug pusher she lived with. While most of the reunions were joyous, this one was tempered with sorrow.

My hometown also got a hard look. Some major changes had come about since my departure. The segregated grade school had been abolished. Blacks could now eat in white restaurants and avoid Jim Crow seating in the two movie theaters. The high school, to its advantage, was at last allowing black students to participate in athletics. Not much else had changed. In the end, my journey into the past was a mixture of nostalgia and depression. The essay, titled "Fort Scott Revisited," was laid out for a cover and twelve pages, then put on a shelf to await publication.

Husband and Wife, Sunday Morning, Fort Scott, 1949

DURING THE LIFE YEARS, I found myself in Los Alamos, a peaceful desert town in New Mexico, where the deadly bomb was being prepared for Hiroshima. En route, in the bus station of a small Texas town, I awaited the army car that was to take me on to Los Alamos. Having recognized me, a white female journalist planted a kiss on my cheek and ran off to board a bus. It was hot. I was drinking from a water fountain when the Texas drawl curled over my head.

"We don't like niggas kissin' white ladies down this way, do we, Bart?"

Angered, I glanced up. Three burly white ruffians were staring at me. Bart was twisting the cord of a venetian blind into a lynch knot. "Nope, Hoagy, and this is what we do to smart-ass darkies who do crazy things like that. Right, Bo?"

"Right, Bart — but we beat the shit out of 'em first. Hangin' ain't a 'nough."

Anger was shoving fear aside. As I stood up I saw one word on a store window across the road — "Gunsmith." Advice from the past was ringing in my ears: "If you hafta go, take somebody with you." Brushing past them I headed for the store.

They followed but stopped outside as I entered the shop.

I spoke to the gunsmith calmly. "I want a loaded .45 automatic pistol."

He looked up at me, then glanced at the three men standing outside the door. "A loaded .45?" He was stalling.

"Yep." He loaded one and handed it to me. I observed him with skepticism. "Where's the firing block? I want to test it."

"Over there in the corner."

I stepped before a thick section of a giant redwood tree, aimed, and pressed the trigger. Nothing happened. "It won't fire. Give me one that will."

He glanced outside. "Did you release the safety?"

"Yep. Give me another one." He did, and I fired two quick bursts as the bullets disappeared into the log. After paying for it I walked toward the door with my finger on the trigger.

They backed away as I came out, but they followed.

"Black bastard! Goddam nigga! Son of a bitch!"

That last insult committed them to a rule ingrained in me since youth. You don't talk bad about somebody's mother unless you're ready to die. I whirled and lifted the gun — just as the army car pulled up. My driver, a military policeman with a gun strapped to his hip, jumped out, spotting the big *Life* logo on my bag. "What in hell's goin' on here?"

"Three crackers giving me a hard time." They stood scowling as I got into the car. We were a mile down the road before I stuck the gun into my camera bag. I had calmed but fright was trembling through me. An innocent kiss had threatened the day with death.

Author's family aboard the *Queen Mary* en route to France, 1950
Photograph by Cecil Layne

PROLONGED FOREIGN ASSIGNMENTS for staff members came slowly. But hardly eighteen months had passed before my orders were marked GO. The destination — Paris once again, but now for two years. My wife, Sally, and our three children, Gordon Jr., David, and our daughter, Toni, would accompany me. The *Queen Mary,* docked at portside, seemed to be waiting with a deck full of promises. Good news came before we sailed. "Fort Scott Revisited" would finally be published while we were en route. But bad news awaited my arrival at the Paris bureau. A major story on General Dwight Eisenhower had forced mine onto the shelf. "That's the end of that," I sighed to my wife. I was right.

Paris, the flower of Europe. For me, a grand feast. No stones had come through our windows when we moved into the white neighborhood. No outpouring of welcome either — just unquestioned acceptance. Immediately I realized why Paul Robeson had said that in Europe he felt like a whole man for the first time; why Richard Wright and his white wife had fled to Paris to escape racial harassment in America; why Dean Dixon, the fine black conductor, had moved to Europe after he was denied work in his homeland; why talented black artists had chosen expatriation. Before long Paris was seducing me with music, literature, and art. Sunday afternoons and evenings were spent at concerts or perhaps a ballet, where I grew to appreciate Bach, Beethoven, Mozart, Prokofiev, Rachmaninoff, and Brahms. I read Proust, Camus, Dostoyevsky, and the poet Pablo Neruda. All this kept me growing in the presence of an unperishing past that had survived the Hun, the Hundred Years War, conflicts with the English, the Black Death, the Prussians, countless revolutions, and two world wars.

At the Café des Deux Magots, I sat where Balzac or Baudelaire might have sat; walked the Rue de la Paix, Place Vendôme, and Montmartre. From above the city in Sacré-Coeur I looked down upon the classical age of Molière; upon Notre-Dame, where Napoleon was crowned emperor. I felt at once younger and older in these inspirational surroundings. I was fleeing forward, lengthening the distance from a blighted past. I needed Paris. I needed Europe.

SOLITUDE

J'y fus marie des ma naissance
Et j'en ai fait ce que j'ai pu.
Ne puis m'y fier
mais je m'y livre
Sans me cacher l'action la pire
ou la pensée.
Recemment dans les froides
heures sordides
C'est devenu la seule chose
Qu'en raisonnant je puisse admettre.

A MATADOR DIED IN MADRID. Young and handsome, he was moving with the grace of a ballet dancer as the bloodied bull charged. His sword was poised for the kill when the beast lunged forward. During that flurried moment its right horn found the matador's groin, tore into it and flung him upward, then viciously trampled him after he struck the ground. The bull was finished off, then the picadores carried their matador from the ring. Estrella, his young widow, was not there. She was home giving birth to their child. As I made my way through the somber crowd, the joyful precelebration ceremony, the matador's triumphant entrance, and his ugly end were suddenly merging as one. Peculiarly, I found myself associating music with the tragedy — elegiac music.

At my home back in Paris, Dean Dixon, the American conductor, stood silently in the hallway listening as I struggled with a passage on the piano. The maid had let him in, but he chose not to interrupt me. After I stopped he entered the parlor. "What was that you were working at?" he asked.

Jokingly I replied, "Oh, the first movement of my piano concerto."

"Very Spanish."

"It's about the death of a bullfighter."

"Could I hear some more?"

"Okay, but I finger it poorly. I was joking about a concerto."

I played some more, and shared some tapes with him. He promised to perform my concerto whenever I finished it. His response stunned me.

"But I've never written a note. I make musical notations with numbers."

He laughed. "So did the ancient composers of China. The important thing is that you can play it. It's easy enough to have it taken down. We'll record you here and send it to Henry Brant in New York. He'll do the dirty work. Keep at it." Six months later a recording of my version of a taped piano concerto was in the hands of Henry Brant. In the months to follow I nearly forgot that I had ever made such a monumental attempt.

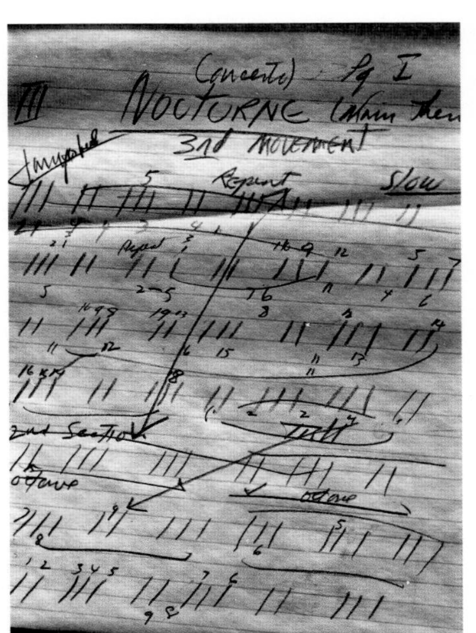

FAR LEFT Author's method of musical notation
LEFT Henry Brant's orchestration of author's piano concerto

ABOVE Bullfight in Madrid, circa 1964
OPPOSITE James Galanos Fashion, circa 1967

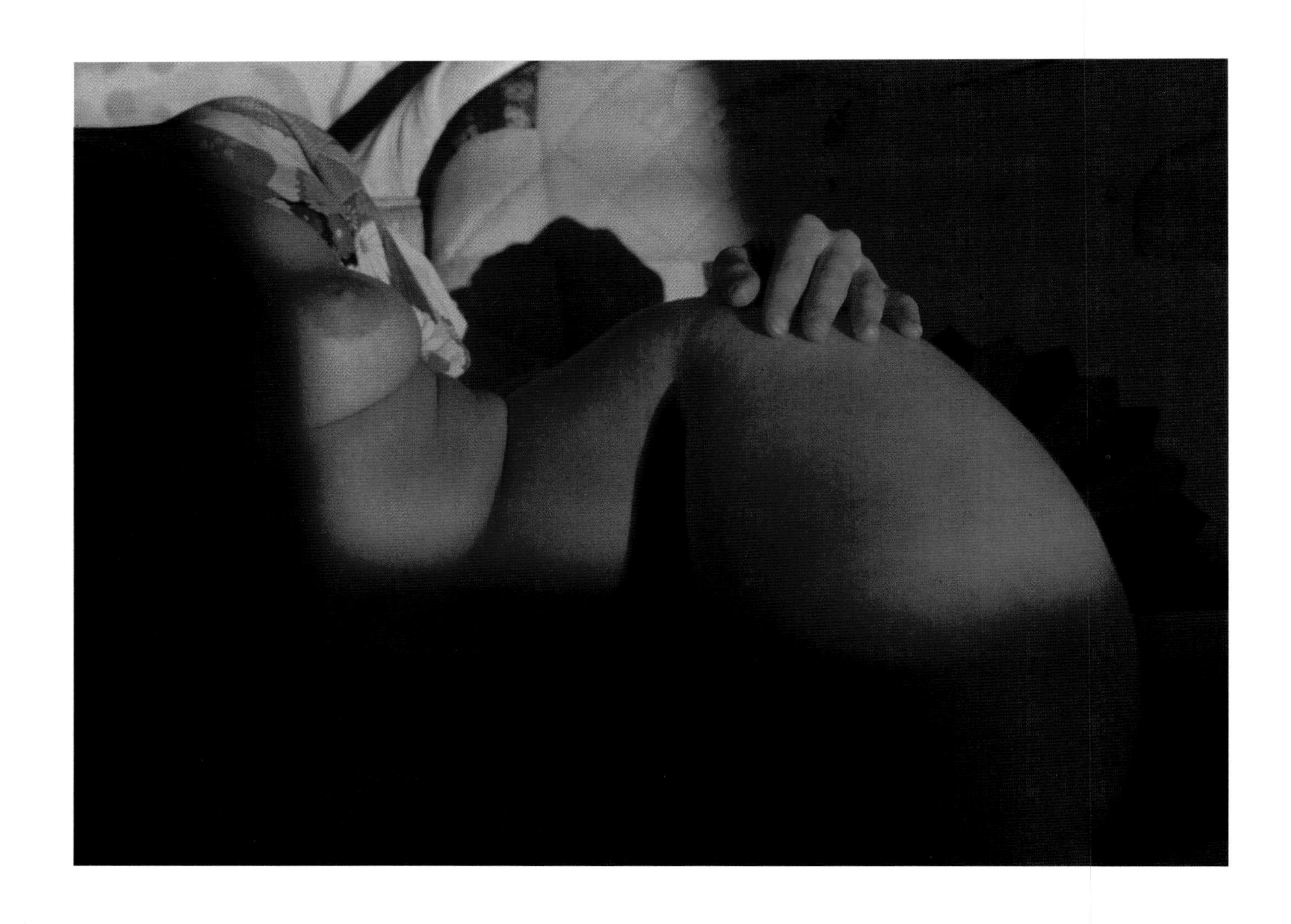

ABOVE Nude, 1965
OPPOSITE Chimney Pots, Paris, 1964

Sleeping Couple, Paris, 1950

NEAR THE SEINE

Rain falls hard over the rue Boissy d'Anglas.
Two young lovers plunge into each other's arms —
lips touching, bodies aflame inside the glow
of their secret sun. A news vendor cries,
"Le gouvernement fout le camp encore!"
Deaf to the Republic's fate they kiss
then move toward the River Seine.
At Pont Neuf two others, crumpled with age,
stand silent in the same downpouring;
neither with a star or dream to offer.
Her troubled cheek twitches.
The wintry hair, like the prickly fur
on her ancient coat, lies slick with wetness.
Sunken into himself, he stands ankle-close,
weighted with time. His wet, left-over coat,
was meant for someone much larger.
Slowly they lift their eyes —
asking to be left in peace.
I, the intruder, hurry off
with confusing poetry rippling inside.

Beggar Man, Paris, 1950

Political Meeting, Paris, 1950

Elderly Woman, Paris, 1950

Otto of Hapsburg's Wedding, 1951

Child in Window,
Paris, 1950

Shopper, Paris, 1950

NATHALIE KOTCHOUBEY, A REPORTER IN THE PARIS BUREAU, and I are in Estoril, Portugal, on assignment. It's beautiful, constantly sunny and steeped in the mannerisms of a tropical resort. During the day we search out and photograph deposed monarchs who have come here to live in luxurious exile. They are a wealthy, spiritless group — King Carol of Romania and his mistress, Magda Lupescu; King Umberto of Italy; Nicholas de Nagybanya Horthy, the Hungarian admiral and statesman; Don Juan de Bourbon, pretender to the Spanish throne, and a few others.

Nathalie, a descendent of Joséphine de Beauharnais, wife of Napoleon I, the daughter of a prince, and a princess in her own right, is an asset to the assignment. Failing to find a notable at home, she discreetly leaves her *petit* calling card, and doors open. Finding them is not too difficult. King Carol spends most of his mornings at a shooting range slaughtering doves, while Lupescu knits on a veranda. Umberto works constantly on his memoirs in his home on a rocky knoll above the sea. Don Juan, a golfer, can be met at the eighteenth hole for a drink at the clubhouse. Horthy spends hours in his Rube Goldberg–like laboratory, doodling at useless inventions. He appears to have gone slightly balmy. Don Juan seems to be the only one working at something beside royalty. Carol seems to be so gracious and gentle, it is difficult to associate him with the infamous assassinations and massacres that took place during his dictatorship. Uncommunicative and morose, Umberto yearns for the throne that was his for a short time after his father, Victor Emmanuel III, died. He yearns in vain. Italy is finished with kings.

Estoril exists in its own particular poetry. Here, strangely wed to the good life, are the poor. Hungered, living close to darkness, they too can be seen at lavish outdoor celebrations where the rich gather. But they are there with their palms lifted upward, begging for daily bread. The rich observe them with silence. On the city's outskirts destitute herdsmen pursue wild horses that roam the wilderness. Some are sold to riding stables; others wind up as meat in marketplaces.

After two weeks we are flying back to Paris. Dawn is now breaking over Estoril. We look down on it — a haven of good life, poverty, genteel boredom, lavish parties, gambling casinos, and make-believe fox hunts. As the city stirs awake, its rejected monarchs are more than likely still asleep. Graying, still clutching their meaningless titles, they lie in my memory like wasted flowers withering away in a royal morgue.

King Carol and Madame Lupescu, Estoril, Portugal, 1950

ABOVE Girl with Baby, Estoril, Portugal, 1950
OPPOSITE Portuguese Boys, Estoril, Portugal, 1950

OPPOSITE Beggar Woman and Child, Estoril, Portugal, 1950
ABOVE Portrait of a Woman, Estoril, Portugal, 1950

ABOVE Wild Horses, Portugal, 1950
OPPOSITE Gambling Woman, 1949

December 15, 1950
Paris is cold. Another heating strike. Today I was at Elsa Schiaparelli's fashion salon photographing the Duchess of Windsor as she selected her spring wardrobe. The Duchess reclined on a satin chaise longue warming under a great mink lap robe. Schiaparelli fawned over her as the mannequins pranced back and forth. Finally the shoes were shown — by a mannequin making her first appearance. Schiaparelli shrugged. "She's ugly as sin, but have you ever seen such gorgeous legs and feet?"

"Beautiful," replied the Duchess.

The mannequin, who didn't understand English, bowed and smiled graciously. Her Highness seemed pleased.

January 3, 1951
Having fled American racism, Richard Wright is now living here in Paris with his wife and daughter. I telephoned him yesterday to invite him for lunch. He accepted and I asked him where he would like to eat. After several moments he said, "You'll probably be shocked, but just for once I'd like to dine at Maxim's." I was shocked — after picturing myself eating with him at a Left Bank bistro and sharing a good bottle of red wine. We both laughed when I revealed my thoughts. Maxim's, with its plush decor, fancy food, and upper class clientele? The last place on the planet I would have expected him to choose.

Having eaten well we were having a cognac when the actress Rita Hayworth came in with Aly Khan and stopped at our table to say hello. When I introduced Wright she gasped, "My God — *the* Richard Wright?"

"None other," I answered. A modest individual, he later expressed surprise that she even knew his name. When the bill came he asked to see it.

"I'm paying, Richard."

"I know that. I just want to see it." He scanned the check. "Good Lord, my family could eat an entire month for that! Let's go have a bottle of cheap wine somewhere."

January 12, 1951
Eisenhower has taken over as Supreme Allied Commander in Europe, and I have been assigned to make a portrait of him.

When I arrived at his headquarters this morning his aides informed me that I would be allowed ten minutes — hardly enough time to unpack my equipment. They were firm. Five minutes more would wreck his schedule. To my dismay, Eisenhower spent ten minutes inspecting my camera. When I complained that my time was gone he went on fondling my camera as though he hadn't heard me. Moments later a major entered. My time was up. Eisenhower waved him away and I spent another half hour photographing him. The general was a camera buff.

January 21, 1951
Looking back over this harrowing day I realize that I have a bad habit of calling on God in times of disaster, then forgetting him until trouble finds me again. Along with a dozen other foreign correspondents, reporter Dodie Hamblin and I were following Eisenhower by chartered plane to NATO countries. We were trailing his Constellation toward Hamburg when his pilot radioed back, warning of dense fog, sleet, heavy snow, and high winds. The general was advising us to turn back. His plane, unlike ours, was equipped with all sorts of sophisticated landing instruments. Our pilot, a Texan who had never flown in Europe before, had only a map, guts, and a dangerous ego. "If Eisenhower's pilot can make it so can I." He flew on toward Hamburg.

Soon we were in the thick of nowhere, unable to see our own wing tips through the dense fog. A great rush of wind, sleet, and snow suddenly struck the windows. And we courageous journalists sat silent and pale. Dodie pressed close to me. Smiling nervously, I took her hand and spoke to God. He didn't respond immediately, and by now most of us were losing our dinner in paper bags. Finally we started down, and as we did, the plane burst into an air pocket, shuddering from the impact. Death crossed my mind, and I waited for it. Then came an unnerving clank of the landing gear locking into position as we dropped lower. Bluish light flashed beneath the wings, darkness, then another flash. Straining against an onrush of sleet and wind, the plane was about to touch down on the icy runway. It struck hard, skidded, lunged forward and came to a halt a few feet short of a concrete wall. We sat silent for a few moments, then a cheer went up for the pilot. I guess God was there for me, despite my momentary forgetfulness.

April 1, 1951
Paris was marred today by a noisy demonstration to save Julius and Ethel Rosenberg, who have been found guilty of espionage and sentenced to death. "They shall not die!" was the refrain of the marchers. A woman with a small child in her arms was struck by a bus as she tried to escape the confusion. The child fell free but the woman's head was smashed flat. The driver covered her body with his coat, then sat on the curb and vomited. Close to the corpse lay a sign. "Vive les Rosenbergs!"

FOLLOWING Officers at Saint-Cyr Military Academy, France, 1951

BELOW Photographers Waiting for Arrival of Dwight D. Eisenhower, Paris, 1951
RIGHT Police at Railway Station in Rome, 1951

POLIZIA
11831

French Soldiers Under Attack, 1951

Rescue at Sea, 1951

Warship at Dawn, 1951

Marshal Pétain's Widow Mourning at His Funeral, 1951

Yeu Island, France, July 23, 1951

Marshal Philippe Pétain was buried on this bleak island this morning, where he had been jailed since 1945 after being convicted of collaborating with the Nazis. DeGaulle had commuted the death sentence to life imprisonment. His widow, heavily veiled, was broken with grief. A procession led by a priest, grim-faced officials, and Yeu's townspeople, accompanied the coffin up a winding road to the edge of the village. It was an unheroic farewell for the once lavishly decorated hero who stopped the Germans at Verdun in 1916 and once served France as its premier. No praiseful obituary; no flag to drape his coffin; no sounding of bugles or rifle fire as they lowered him into the earth. Only a few consoling words from an aged priest, advising the widow to keep her own life moving.

I remained at the burial site until everyone had gone except two gravediggers. They ate their lunch, then, smiling contempt for the dead traitor, tossed the scraps into the dark space where the coffin lay. After observing me curiously for a moment they began shoveling in dirt. The discarded hero was left to rot.

Marshal Pétain's Funeral Procession, 1951

Mourner at Marshal Philippe Pétain's Funeral, 1951

Elizabeth Campbell Parks, author's second wife, at premiere of *The Learning Tree,* New York City, 1968
Photograph by Warner Brothers, Seven Arts

January 15, 1952
Paris is suddenly akin to a broken dream. After two fine years there, I am back in America and I smell blood. Racism is still in the air, and black people, angry, tired of waiting, are demanding its departure. How often have I heard the white man say, "I know the Negro"? No one knows the black man, not even the black man. All our lives we have cloaked our feelings, bided our time, waited for the year, the month, the day, and the hour when we could do what we are doing right now — looking our oppressor squarely in the eye and telling him what we think, what we want, and what we intend to get.

Our young people are saying boldly that they will not go on suffering while the white man insists on slow surrender through law and time. Speak to these young black people of new laws and legislation and they answer: "If some whites are sincere, they will raise their voices against the racists." Tell them that times are changing and they answer: "We are changing the times!"

June 26, 1952
A cable from Paris arrived: my first piano concerto will get its performance in Venice within the month. Incredible! Dean Dixon kept his word. Vivian, his wife, will be at the piano.

Two weeks later I flew to Venice. The concert was moved from the Opera House to the courtyard of the Doges' Palace. En route to the festivities in a gondola, Vivian, Dean, and I waved at well-wishers who tossed flowers from the waterside. One shouted "Bravo, Maestro! Bravo!" Dean touched me and smiled. "He means you, my friend. Wave to him."

Just moments away my first musical work was about to be performed by a symphony orchestra under a moonlit sky. Henry Brant had done the "dirty work." Now Dean Dixon would bring fulfillment to my efforts. Nervously I watched him approach the podium. After a slight pause his baton shot upward. The first chord sent a flock of pigeons skyward. From that moment on, I was akin to a zombie — hearing yet not hearing, seeing but not seeing. The night, the music, became one huge blur as the four movements echoed through one ear and out the other. The last chord sounded. Applause rang in my ears but I sat like a stone. A woman's hand touched my shoulder. "The conductor is motioning for you to stand up." I rose stiffly, bowed, and sat down. It was a golden, joyful evening.

But that joy would be tempered with family problems when I returned to America. My marriage to Sally had been gradually falling apart, and within six months we were filing for a divorce. Having given up the difficult task of trying to understand me or her three children, she bid a sorrowful farewell to us and departed.

In the next few years a loneliness began spreading its presence. Things were at their worst when Elizabeth Campbell, an exquisitely beautiful young lady, eased into my life. Sensing that being in love was my nature, she gently led me to another marriage altar. Our daughter, Leslie, was born two winters later. Her features, closely akin to those of her mother, left me filled with joy. I lived to watch, touch, and love her as she flowered like a rose.

Keyboard, 1981

Color Gallery I

SENSUOUS, HEROIC, ENCHANTING, EXQUISITE, GARISH. Just a few descriptions assigned to the word *color* by a book of worthy definitions. There were more than a hundred others, but I would add several more — smoky, misty, or why not rainfallish? Vigorous color lies in such omissions. I remember smoke adrift above the volcano on Stromboli; mist crawling low over the North Sea; silver rain falling on Peruvian mountain peaks. When these delicate blessings appeared, I hurriedly attempted to record them before they dropped into a hole of my memory. The spirit of color dwells within the subject matter, which is unending. Perhaps that justifies the multitude of definitions. Yet, I often find myself preoccupied with several that were omitted.

I tend to use color when it dominates, while certain photographers feel that only black-and-white expresses the real truth of their subject matter. But I have, at times, found color to be even more acceptable to the eye. While my approach to each medium is somewhat different, I realize that both knock at my door with the same purpose. Only when they knock together do they confuse me. Then a wild guess picks the one I was waiting for.

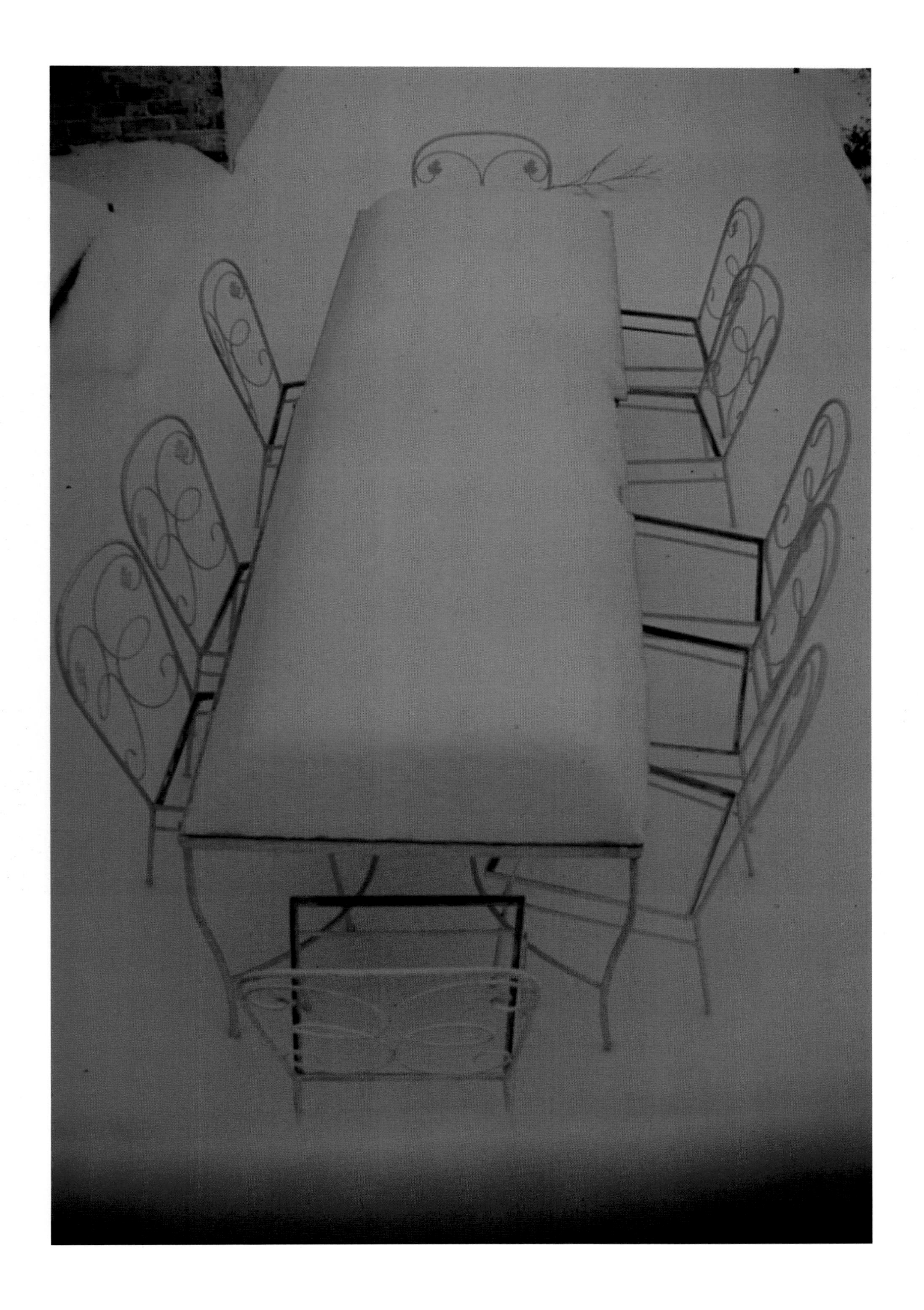

VICTOR
PAZ
horas 18 y 30 HOY
Fiel a Bolivar
y a su Pueblo
EN EL PASADO, EN EL PRESENTE
Y EN EL PORVENIR
VOTE POR EL
gloria
UNZAGA

Vivienne
London

P
SOSTA PERMESSA
60 MINUTI

TEKNE
la nuova Olivet

Segregation in the South

NOTES FROM A DIARY: It's 1956. I'm in Shady Grove, a black section of Choctaw County, Alabama. My assignment, "Segregation in the Deep South," has kept me driving around the state of Alabama for nearly two weeks. Night has fallen in this dusty countryside where I just escaped a band of hostile white men who are searching for me. I backed away from several situations earlier after being warned that these men were awaiting my arrival. I realize now that their informant is the same person who was assigned to assist me down here. I'm lying in hiding in the darkness of a shanty owned by black woodcutter Willie Causey, whose family I've chosen as the centerpiece of this assignment. And while the family sleeps, my thoughts swirl around the tragedies that brought me here. Just a few miles down the road Klansmen are burning and shooting blacks and bombing their churches. Southland is afire, and lying here in the dark, hunted, I feel death crawling the dusty roads. The silence is spattered with fear.

I fled Choctaw County over a back road two nights later. After reaching Birmingham at dawn I took the first plane to New York. Not until it roared upward did I breathe easily.

When my story was published a month later, the sparse comforts of Willie Causey's family self-destructed like buckshot. The same Choctaw County citizens who had hunted for me stripped Willie of all his possessions and then, using brutal restraints, ran him and his wife and six children out of town with a threat ringing in his ears: "It's the rope for you if you try comin' back!" In New York, a collect call from Willie informed me of his plight. *Life* acted promptly, sending the family $25,000 to help them resettle in another part of the South. Two of the magazine's editors, Hugh Moffet and Richard Stolley, went to Choctaw County with the hope of getting Willie's property returned to him. Several men with shotguns stood outside the mayor's house when they arrived. Mrs. Rosie McPhearson, a spirited, wealthy widow who ran things around the county, was there, too, and she was blunt: "It's burrheads like Willie that's causing trouble for the whites. . . . We ought to ship every one of them back to Africa." One of the men left the editors with these parting words: "That nigger that took those pictures is mighty damn lucky. If we'd caught him he woulda been tarred and feathered."

Looking back now to the black revolution of the 1960s, I realize why we refused to wait for justice any longer—especially from the Supreme Court. Only after a long struggle did it outlaw school segregation, but even then black children would still be harrassed by white mobs before entering school. Even then Federal troops had to be brought in to escort them to their desks, while "Lynch 'em!" thundered through the corridors. When Rosa Parks was jailed for not giving her seat to a white man on an Alabama bus, the sit-ins would arrive. As one group wiped away blood and spit, another one walked in to suffer more blood and spit. When the Freedom Riders began their terror-filled forays into the deepest South, their buses were firebombed, their windows smashed, tires slashed, and their young Riders beaten. A bomb exploded inside a Birmingham church and four black children died. In

Mississippi a white Southerner aimed his gun at the back of Medgar Evers, the civil rights leader, and hit his mark. White police waited with clubs, guns, water hoses, and dogs to wreak havoc on his mourners. But armed only with our blackness against this violence, we would keep marching on.

Willie Causey and Family, Shady Grove, Alabama

MAY

DRINK
Coca-Cola
So Mild
So Good
CAVALIER
FLAVOR...
MILDNESS
Sunbeam Bread
Sunbeam
ENERGY-PACKED
BREAD

DAIRY QUEEN
Butterscotch
Banana
Split
PLASTIC FOOD KEEPER
DAIRY QUEEN
Butter Pecan
COLORED
ONLY
HOT DOG
Western Sauce

Crime

MY ASSIGNMENT: EXPLORE CRIME ACROSS AMERICA. A journey through hell. I started in Chicago — a mecca for drug addiction, murder, and corruption. The year was 1957. I rode with detectives through shadowy districts, climbed fire escapes, broke through windows and doors with them. Brutality was rampant. Violent death showed up from dawn to dawn. Vile language was the prose, even in the presence of young children caught up in the brutal confrontations. I sorrowed for two small girls who stood screaming as their father was pistol-whipped by a cop. A few hours before, this same enforcer had admitted that he could have been a crook or a cop. For him it had been "a toss-up." Before kicking his way through the door he had shocked me. "If you want I'll put a bullet in some bastard's ass when we go in. It'll make a good picture."

"No, thanks."

One detective showed a tinge of mercy during a raid. He wrapped the head of a sledgehammer with a towel before attacking a suspect with it. Back at the precinct another detective took a needle and vial from a drawer and led me to a cell of an inmate who lay on a cot. "Here, Joe, take a shot for this man. He wants a picture of a junkie." Happy to accommodate, Joe put a belt around his forearm, found a large vein, and sent the dope home. I got my picture, but a sense of guilt still lingers inside me.

One encounter in particular stays on in my memory. Inmate Hudson's cell on San Quentin's death row was terribly quiet. He had one night to live. At dawn he would pay his debt for knifing a boy to death.

"Mr. Hudson, had you ever seen the boy before?" I asked.

"Nope. Just a little pissed off at the time. The undertaker I worked for never let me cut on a corpse. I don't know — maybe a book I read called *The Big Knife* had something to do with it."

"How do you feel about dying?"

"I'm sure not happy about it. You coming to watch me go?"

"Would you like for me to be there?"

"Yep, to say a little prayer for me."

Twelve of us and a cocky young guard are standing silent in the safe quarter of this pale green gas chamber. Now, for some unaccountable reason, the guard is motioning me down front — to within three feet of the chair. Only thick glass separates me from the death I am about to witness. Behind me a minister leafs through his Bible for words to deliver at the appropriate time. The door to the death cubicle is opening, and I damn myself for being here. It's too late for that. The doomed man is approaching the chair, ashen, shaking, and flanked by three guards. The whispering of the minister stirs the silence. "That the saying of Jesus might be fulfilled, which he spoke, signifying what death he should die." The prisoner observes us through tears, his eyes seeming to question our presence. Now, turning slowly, he is using up every precious moment before surrendering to the chair. "Then said Pilate unto them, 'Take ye him, and judge him according him to your own law.' The Jews therefore said unto him, 'It is not lawful for us to put any man to death.'" He inhales deeply as they strap down his shoulders and legs. Two guards are leaving. One lingers to adjust a stethoscope over the heart. "The Lord is my shepherd; I shall not want. He maketh me to lie down in green pastures; he leadeth me beside the still waters." Before leaving, the guard pats the prisoner's back and thrusts a Bible into his hands. Now he sits alone. A tear drops to his cheek as he thumbs through Samuel, Kings, Chronicles, and Ezra. "He restoreth my soul; he leadeth me in the paths of righteousness for his name's sake." The warden's arm is rising. "Yea, though I walk through the valley of the shadow of death, I will fear no evil: for thou art with me; thy rod and thy staff they comfort me." The warden's arm drops; the pellet drops. The gas is rising. His head snaps backward. The Bible falls to the floor and snaps shut. Intense quivering descends from the top of his head to his belly, his hips, his legs, and, with a final spasm, his toes. He is forever still. "And I will dwell in the house of the Lord forever."

He had murdered dispassionately; his judgment was served dispassionately. I fail to distinguish the profanity of one act from the profanity of the other. One evil, cloaked in cold judicial morality, has just fed upon another.

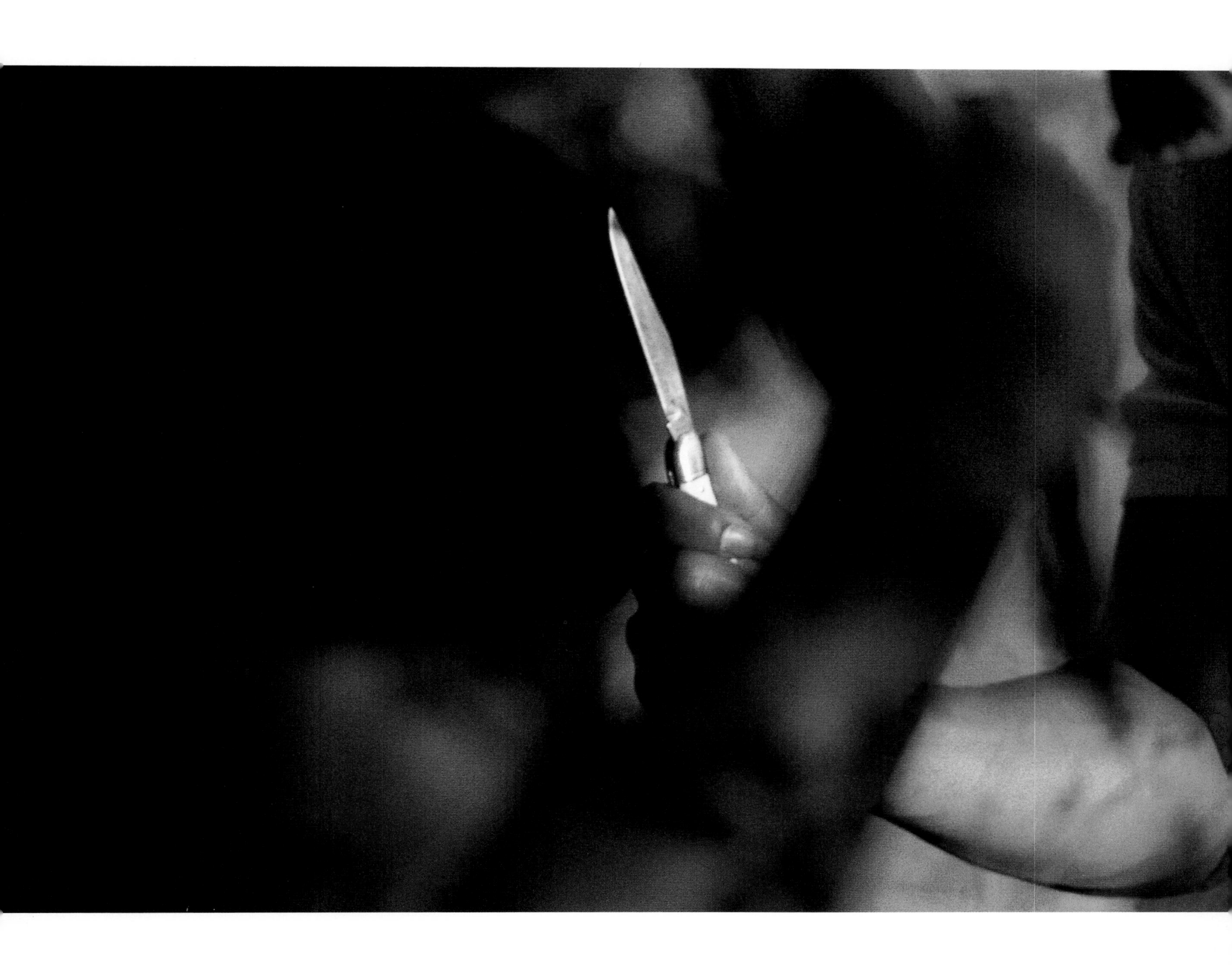

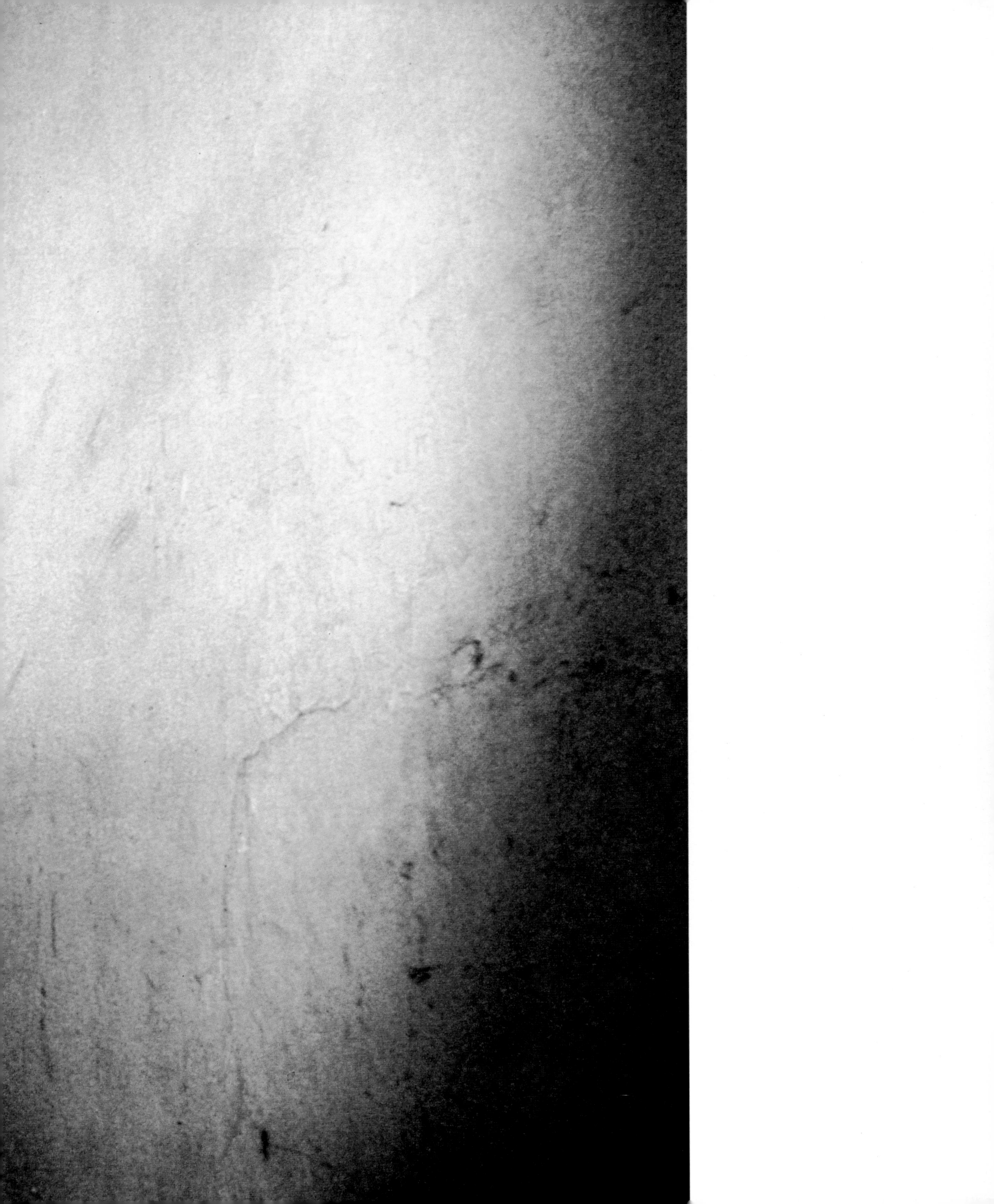

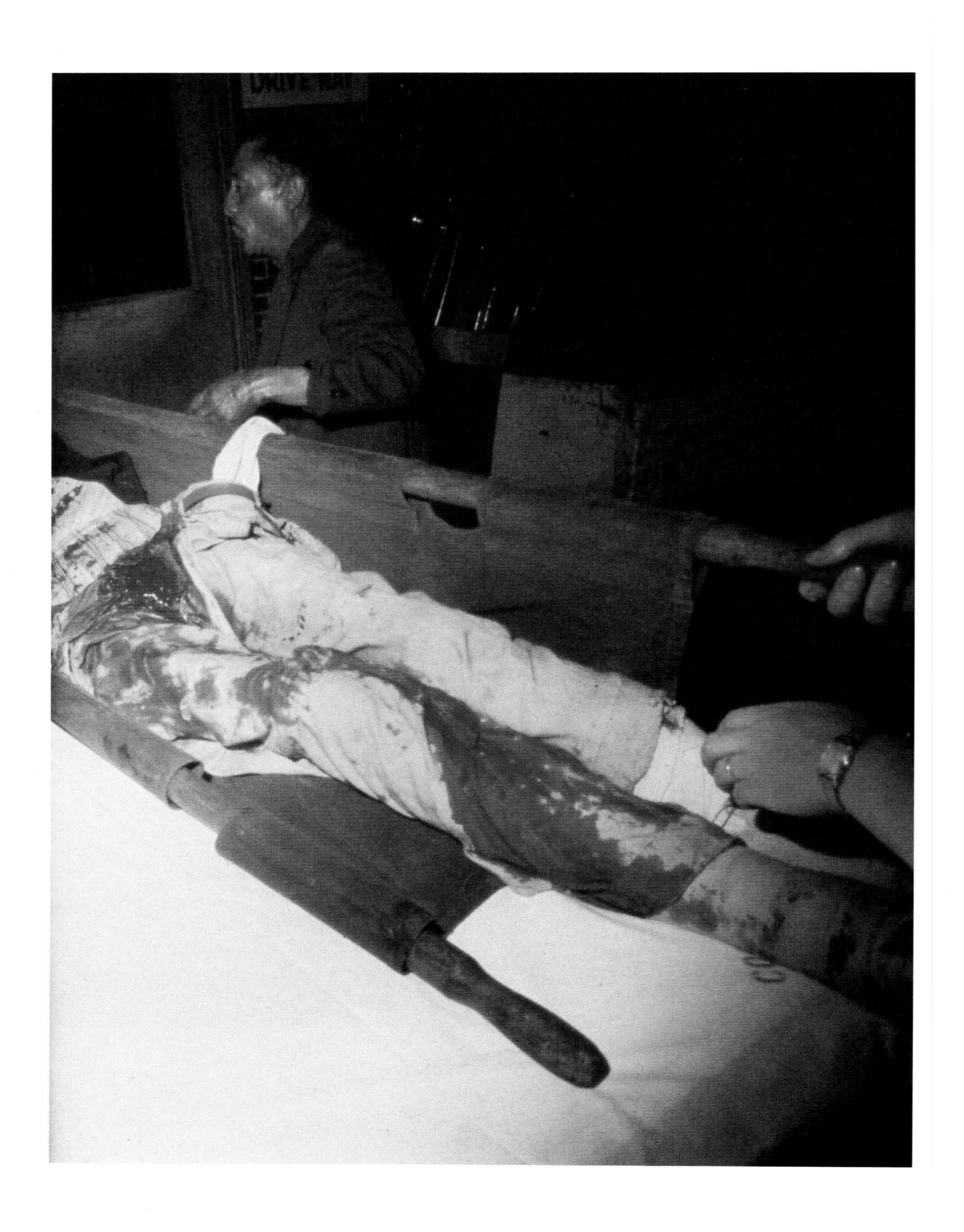

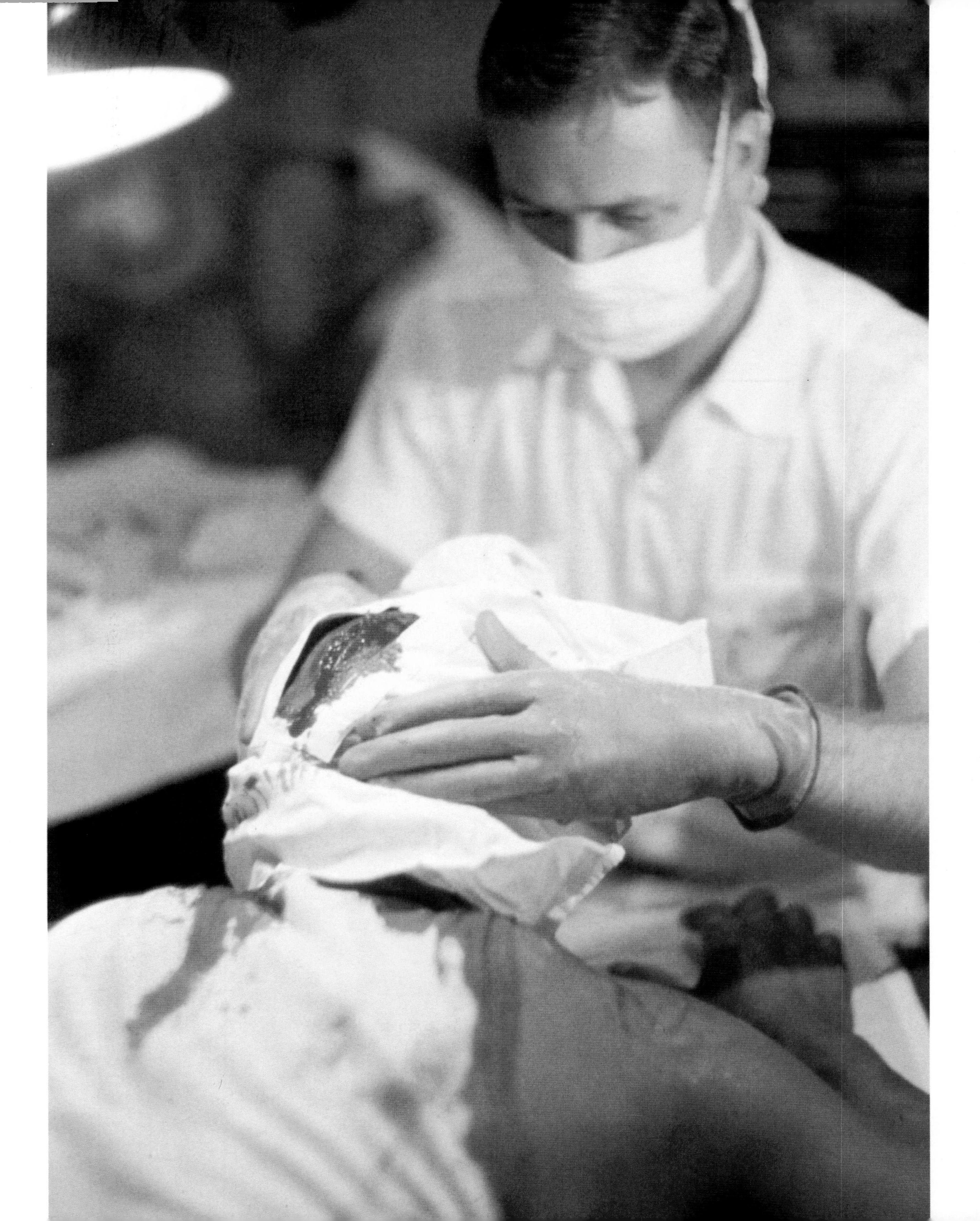

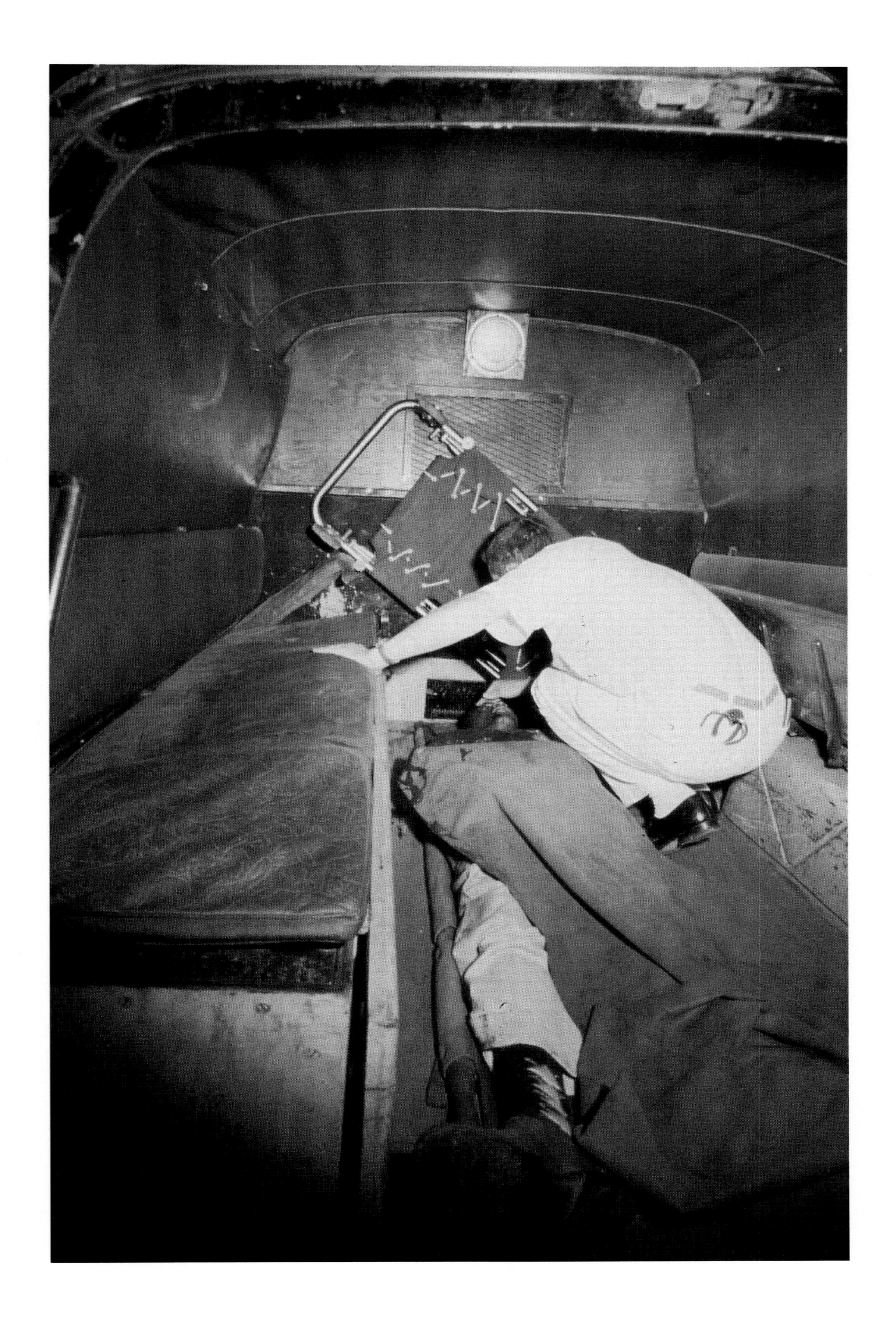

GRAND ST.
ONE WAY

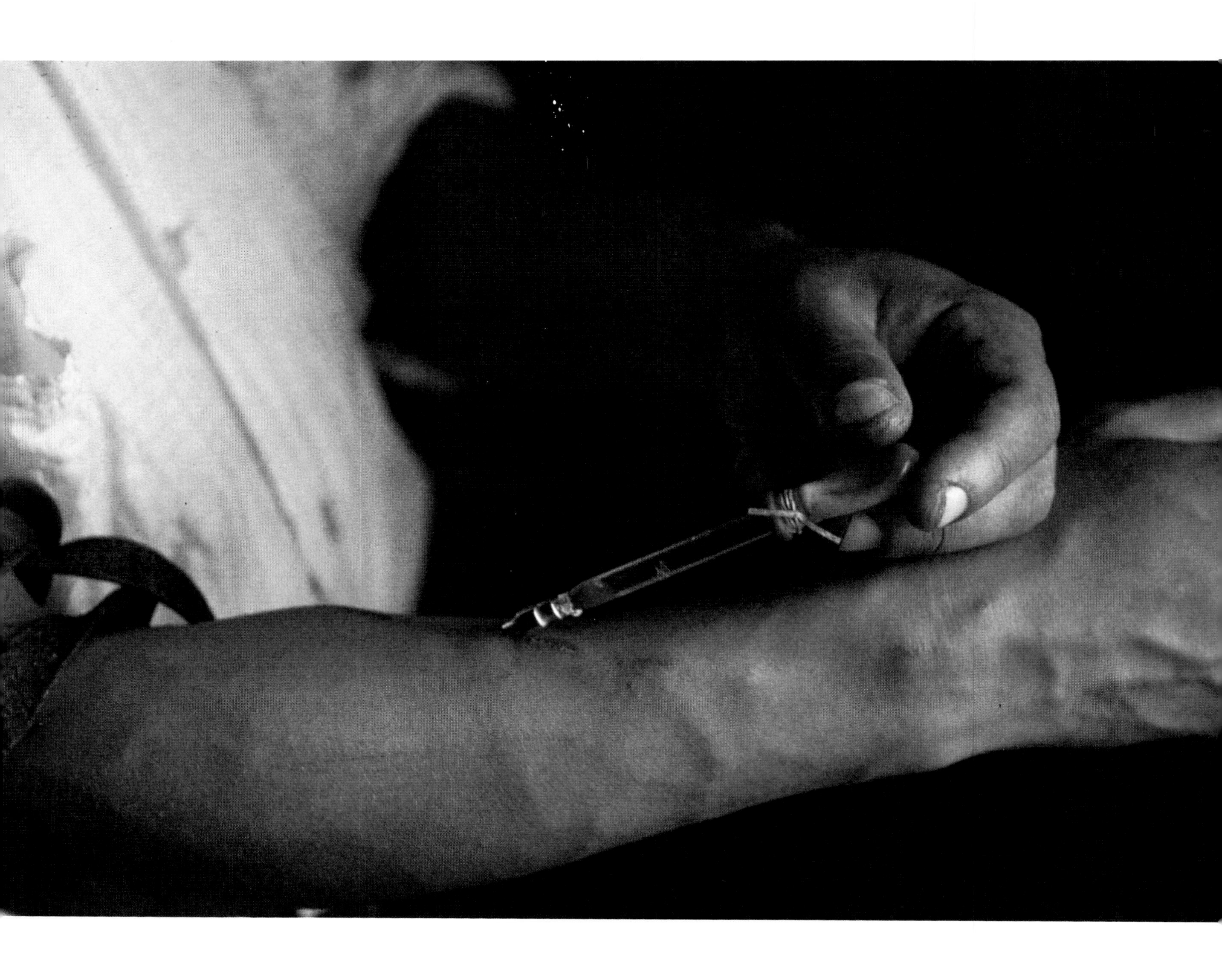

Duke Ellington

SOMEWHERE IN EUROPE, while thumbing the pages of Oxford's *Shorter English Dictionary on Historical Principles,* I ran across these items — written, revised, and edited by C. T. Onions and other erudite fellows.

Negro: An individual (especially a male), one distinguished by black skin, woolly hair, flat nose and thick protruding lips

Music: A fine art concerned with the combination of sounds with a view to beauty of form and the expression of feeling

Jazz: Syncopated music played by Negro bands in the U.S.

In my opinion, these unenlightened fellows dressed up as learned historians revealed their own biased sufferings. I wouldn't have trusted any of them to define much of anything, especially jazz. To them, the true meaning of the word was as evasive as silence. Caught up in a mixture of intellect and stupidity they failed to understand this impassioned art that slices one's senses into so many delicate patterns. However, for multitudes, one definition remains sufficient.

Jazz: Edward Kennedy Ellington, also Duke, Red, Duc, or Ducem.

He had one main mistress. She was as old as the sun but, to him, as "beautiful as a full moon over sea mist." Her name: Music. So often Edward composed with Billy Strayhorn at his side. "Sweet Pea is my alter ego," he would say. This was his high praise for the sensitive young arranger who, with quiet enthusiasm, helped purify Ellington's finest works. Like his music, Edward's humor could also emerge with graceful subtlety. He, Harry Carney, and I were approaching San Francisco by car as he slept in the backseat. It was dawn, and in the distance the city's famous bridge looked to be adrift in fog. Harry called to him. "Wake up, Duke. There's a scene up ahead you could put to music." Edward awoke, gazed at the spectacle for several moments, and mumbled, "Damn — a floating bridge. Those white architects are sure getting smart." Then, with more beauteous music in his dreaming, he fell asleep again.

Duke Ellington with Arranger Billy Strayhorn, Los Angeles, 1960

Flavio da Silva

IN 1961 I FOUND MYSELF dead center of the worst poverty I have ever encountered — in the favela of Catacumba, a desolate mountainside of misery outside Rio de Janeiro. In Portuguese the word *catacumba* means "death." For thousands of Brazilians trapped there, it amounted to death. Burning sun baked the dank mud rot. Flies swarmed over garbage. Human excrement clogged open sewers twisting down through a maze of wooden shacks. Just a few miles beyond them was a sparkling lagoon and, in the far distance lining the beautiful oceanfront, were the gleaming white homes of the rich.

Folded into my back pocket was the assignment: "Poverty in Latin America." I had stopped to rest in the shade of a jacaranda tree when José Gallo, a *Life* reporter and my interpreter, sat down beside me. Weary from the steep ascent, we watched as the small boy climbed toward us with a tin of water on his head. He wore a pair of filthy denim shorts, and he was miserably thin with spindly legs. Death was all over him — in his sunken eyes, cheeks, and jaundiced coloring. He stopped for a moment to cough, smiled a smile I won't forget, and continued climbing.

Instantly, this frail boy struggling up the mountainside became the subject of my coverage. We followed him, stopping whenever he stopped, until he reached home — a crumbling one-room wooden shack. He entered and shut the door. Gallo knocked softly, and a thin voice screeched, *"Silencio! Silencio!"* The door was opened, and he stood smiling with a crying, naked baby under his arm. Smacking the child's rump, he rattled something off in Portuguese.

Gallo turned to me. "His name is Flavio and he's asking us in." As we entered, Flavio screamed at a younger boy whom we assumed was his brother. Then he tossed the baby onto the bed between two small girls and motioned for us to sit down. There were only two boxes and one bed. Two girls burst into the shack screaming at each other. The bigger one, about Flavio's size, began pounding on the smaller one, who looked to be about eight years old. Flavio stepped in to part them, only to receive a glob of spit in his face from the larger one, who then fled back out the door. Smiling, Flavio wiped away the spit and began explaining.

"These are my brothers and sisters." Pointing them out, he said, "That's Mario, the bad one. That's Luzia, who thinks she's pretty, and that's Albia and Isabel on the bed with the baby. His name is Zacarias. I'm the oldest. Maria, who just ran out the door, is next to me. Baptista, my other brother, is at the bottom of the hill with Poppa and Momma. She's washing clothes, and Poppa sells kerosene."

My eyes moved over the shack — a patchwork of misshapen boards with large gaps, precariously propped against the mountainside; a rotting floor with a hole for a toilet; a baby's crib; and a small wooden table held together with wire. A makeshift stove, made from the top of a discarded gas range, resting on bricks and tin; a dented old tea kettle and a cooking pot charred black from flames. This was home for the ten da Silvas.

"Americano." The kids gazed at me, pulled at my pockets, and touched my camera. Now

and then one would poke a finger into my ribs or pinch my arm, then wait for a reaction. By the time Maria returned, Flavio had started a fire in the stove and put on a pot of beans. He seemed to have forgotten the spit. "Stir the beans," he said curtly. She was pretty and seemed to know it. As she began stirring she watched us with mischief in her eyes. Mario, with angry eyes, sat on the floor, pounding it viciously with an iron bar. "Stop it, fool!" Flavio shouted. Mario's eyes burned into his brother's. "I mean it!" Flavio said, thumping his head. Mario continued pounding the floor with the bar. Flavio turned on him. "Git up, you lazy pig, and move the trash out front!"

"Fuck you!" Mario snapped. Then he jumped up and ran out the door. A scream came from outside. We hurried out to see Mario clutching his leg and crying.

"What's the matter?" Flavio asked.

"A dog bit me!"

"Aha! Good enough for you, you lazy pig." He turned to Maria. "Get the alcohol." When she brought it he poured some on the wound. Mario howled.

"Quiet, you pig! Quiet! I bet you bit the poor dog first." He then took Mario by the ear. "Now get rid of that trash like I told you." Mario obeyed. Flavio then washed some rice in a saucepan, scooped out the grains, and transferred them to the charred pot. The dirty water wasn't to be wasted. He tossed in a chunk of lye soap and ordered the children to wash their hands. After they finished, he splashed the water onto the floor, dropped to his knees, and began scrubbing.

As Flavio left the shack he cautioned Maria, "Don't let the rice burn. If Poppa beats me, you get it later." Happy to get at the licking spoon, she stirred for a few moments, dipped out a spoonful of beans, and ate them. Luzia was watching. "I saw you," she said. "I'm going to tell on you."

"You bitch!" Luzia threw a stick at Maria and ran out of the shack. Zacarias, the baby, fell asleep. Mario slouched in a corner sucking his thumb. Isabel and Albia sat on the floor clutching each other with a strange tenderness. Isabel held on to Albia's hair, and Albia clutched at Isabel's neck.

Flavio returned with an armful of kindling wood and dumped it beside the stove. After resting for a few moments, he went down the mountainside for more water. Dusk had arrived when he finally returned. He had taken on the look of an old man. Plainly it was he who kept the family going.

By the time Nair and José da Silva arrived with Baptista, Gallo and I felt we had become part of their family. Flavio had told them about us when he went back for more water. Nair was thickset with wavy, brown hair, pale blue eyes, and a sharp nose. Her stomach was swollen with another child. Silently she acknowledged us with a sad, toothless smile. She wore a long, crinkled black skirt and a faded gingham blouse. Her heavy hands and arms were pale from washing clothes. The bare calloused feet had lost their shape. Zacarias scrambled off the bed to go to her. Tired beyond speaking, she slumped upon a box and gently patted his behind.

José, the father, after viewing us with skepticism, managed a curt hello. Barefoot, dressed in baggy trousers and a ragged shirt, he was a portrait of gloom. His Indian ancestry showed in his black, wiry hair. After ordering Flavio to hurry with dinner, he sat on a box scowling at the holes in the ceiling. Baptista, a handsome boy of about seven, sat at his father's feet. He had his father's color, with deep-set eyes that seemed to gaze without blinking. His calmness set him apart from his brothers and sisters.

Flavio's scurrying about showed fear of his father. When dinner was ready, José da Silva took his place in the center of the bed with his legs crossed beneath him. The others gathered around him. There was only one huge tin platter. Flavio filled it with beans and rice, then put it before his father. Using one of the two spoons he owned, José began to eat. After chewing for a few moments he nodded for the others to start. They joined in, eating with their fingers. Finally Flavio served himself some food on a tin plate, then pushed it toward us. We refused. He smiled.

José da Silva didn't ask why I wanted to photograph his family; nor did he seem to care. But suddenly he began complaining. "I've got a bad back. I make about twenty dollars a month selling kerosene and bleach. My wife washes clothes for people. It takes money for us to keep going." He frowned. "My back tells me there's bad weather tomorrow. And there's no money for a doctor."

It was late when we left. Zacarias was asleep in his crib. All the others had collapsed in a heap and sprawled across one another. Space was reserved for José on the near side. At the foot of the bed lay Flavio. As we bade José da Silva goodnight, Flavio fell into a spasm of coughing so violent his lungs seemed to be tearing apart.

Gallo and I made our way slowly down the dark path as three men climbed toward us.

"Try not to look like a stranger. The favela's dangerous at night," Gallo said softly. "Lots of thugs and robbers. Even the police stay away after dark." As the men passed us, one grabbed my arm and demanded a cigarette. Gallo pulled me on. "Don't come up here alone at night. If you do, stay at the da Silvas' until morning."

After Catacumba, my hotel room on the Copacabana waterfront seemed oversized. The entire da Silva shack would have fit into one corner. I ordered a steak for dinner, but halfway through it I thought of the stale rice and beans. My appetite vanished. There was no doubt now. Flavio da Silva was my story.

The following morning I filed the longest cable of my life — all about Flavio and the favela of Catacumba. Forty-eight hours passed before the response from my story editor, Tim Foote, arrived: LOOKS LIKE YOU'RE ON TOP OF A GREAT STORY — FLAVIO SOUNDS TRAGIC BUT HE SOUNDS WONDERFUL. . . . KEEP A DIARY.

March 22, 1961
We reached the shack at 9:30 this morning. Albia and Isabel were swinging in a dirty hammock hung across the room. Flavio was warming leftovers for the children's breakfast. I stepped back to take a picture of the hammock and upset the cooking pot. Flavio's laughter left him so weak he had to sit down for several minutes. After regaining strength he scraped the leftovers off the floor and put them into the pot. Guilt and regret poured through me as I watched. This kid is dying. We have to get him to a doctor.

March 23, 1961
Unlike Flavio, his brothers and sisters are unpredictable. I'm "Gorduun" to them now. Albia or Isabel wiggle beneath my arms, grip my fingers tightly and remain close for several minutes. Still it's not surprising when one or the other sticks me with a nail. They seem to be testing my response to their inner feelings. Nair doesn't have time to give them love; their father seems incapable. So any hands that touch with gentleness are dear. To ignore them for long is to abuse them, and their reaction is anger.

March 26, 1961
Flavio was standing beside the shack gazing toward the white buildings in the far distance when we arrived this morning. Although he is twelve he has never been to the Copacabana Beach or downtown Rio. I had brought a large fish. He took it inside and ordered Maria to clean it. She was knifing away the guts when Luzia touched the tail.

Maria slapped her face with the wet fish. When Luzia started crying, Flavio grabbed the fish and slapped Maria's face with it. She was going for his back with the knife when I grabbed her wrist. Wrenching free, she came at me with the knife. I spun her about, took the knife, and held her tightly for a few moments. Surprisingly, she looked up at me, pleading, "Money, Gorduun! Money, money!"

"Maria, stop begging!" Flavio shouted. A plane roared over the favela. He looked up toward the sound. "I would like to fly on that big bird some day."

March 27, 1961
It was terribly hot today. José da Silva, looking more dead than alive, lay feverish and groaning underneath the dirty blanket. Little Isabel watched as a huge black spider crawled over him. When it reached his knee, she smashed it with her fist. José shrieked and his hand shot up and smacked her. She stood crying until Flavio dunked some bread into coffee and shoved it into her mouth. Then, for no apparent reason, she turned on Zacarias and kicked him in the head. In the baby's defense, Luzia shoved Isabel to the floor. Mario hit Isabel, and Flavio struck him. Isabel, her sullen wet eyes on Luzia, sat in a corner muttering, "Bitch! Bitch!" Luzia went outside, doubled herself up on the ground and began sucking her thumb. Each day is nightmarish.

March 28, 1961

Last week, a senator for the district came to Catacumba to answer a complaint from a woman living next door to the da Silvas. "My daughter's dead for three days," she complained. "And no one brings a death certificate so I can bury her. Come. See for yourself."

We followed him into the shack. The temperature was over ninety, but neighbors had kept the shack reasonably cool with sides of cardboard boxes that kept the sun out. The bier was made of wooden crates. A child fanned away flies with large leafy branches. The headrest was a board with candles burning on each end of it. The pillow for her head and a sheet for a shroud were amenities few favelados received during life. Having been lent by a laundress, they belonged to her client. A hand towel had been placed under the dead woman's chin and knotted at the top of her head to keep the mouth closed.

The senator explained matters. "This is a weekend. The coroner is probably on vacation. I'll do what I can." The certificate came two days later. The corpse was carried down Catacumba by four neighbors.

April 3, 1961

On Saturday night I sat at the sidewalk café at my hotel watching young prostitutes bargain with men. A pretty girl with sad eyes approached me. "Like fun, Señor? It is very cheap. I need money for my brothers and sisters."

I thought of the da Silva kids and gave her some cruzeiros. Then, ignoring Gallo's advice, I took a taxi to the foot of Catacumba. Far up into the mountainside's darkness I became apprehensive and climbed cautiously. Farther up, I lost all sense of direction and bypassed the path leading to the da Silva's. I came to a shack where a man sat in a doorway. *"Boa noite,"* I said. "I'm trying to find the path to the da Silva place."

He pointed into the darkness. "You just come by it. Go few feet to left then to right." I thanked him and turned back.

Flavio was having a bad night. I could hear him coughing as I approached the shack. Nair let me in. Flavio sat on a box by a kerosene lamp inhaling steam from a pan of hot water. All the others were asleep. Nair slumped in fatigue. I motioned for her to go to bed. Before lying down, she poured a portion of clear liquid into a tin cup, then added cold coffee. After stirring the mixture with a finger, she put it to Flavio's lips. Grimacing, he drank it. He finally fell asleep and I lifted him into bed at the feet of the others. A sniff of the liquid Nair had poured into the cup told me it was kerosene.

I lay on the floor, hearing the family's snoring in uneven rhythms punctuated by Flavio's coughing. An hour passed before I fell into an uneasy sleep. By seven o'clock the following morning Flavio was already up, tiptoeing about, preparing a breakfast of stale coffee and chunks of hard bread. He looked down at me and smiled. And I wondered why he smiled.

April 7, 1961
Gallo and I took Flavio to the clinic at the bottom of the favela this morning. It was much larger than the shacks that surrounded it. He sat on a bench between us. "What will the doctor do to me?" he asked.

"We'll wait and see," Gallo answered. There was only one doctor, and a large gathering of patients were ahead of us. Most were barefoot with bleeding sores on their feet and legs. An hour passed before the doctor — a large, pink-jowled man — began the examination. "Open your mouth. Say 'Ah.' Jump up and down. Breathe in. Breathe out. Take off those pants. Bend over. Stand up. Cough. Louder. Cough again." Finally he gave Flavio some pills and a bottle of cough syrup. Then he took Gallo and me into an outer room. "This little fellow has been here before. He's living on borrowed time. He belongs to José, the kerosene dealer, doesn't he?"

"Yes."

"What interest do you have in him?"

"We want to help in some way."

"Too late. The child's already wasted with bronchial asthma, malnutrition, and, I suspect, tuberculosis. Heart, lungs, and teeth are all bad. Sorry I can't be more encouraging." We thanked him and left.

"What did he say inside?" Flavio asked as we started up the hill.

"Nothing to worry about, Flav," Gallo answered. "You're going to be all right."

"I'm not afraid of death, but I worry about my brothers and sisters."

"You're going to be all right, Flav. Don't worry."

April 9, 1961
This was the day I promised Flavio and Mario their first trip to Copacabana Beach. They were eagerly waiting at the entrance to the favela when Gallo and I arrived in his car. Except for their soiled, tattered pants, they were naked. The two of them sat close together in the backseat. After passing the gleaming white buildings, the vast Copacabana Beach came into view. "Look! Look, Flavio!" Mario cried. Hundreds of multicolored umbrellas cast pools of shade over the sand. Children were flying colorful kites. "Is this here all the time?"

"Yes, yes, of course," Flavio shouted. On the beach they joined hands and warily approached the water's edge. When a wave broke against their legs they scurried back to shore. It took a few minutes before they would wade the foaming surf without fear. Later I bought them food. When it was time to go back, they sat silent as we took a final sweep along the sea. For them it was akin to a visit to heaven. En route to Catacumba, we stopped at a grocery store and bought enough food to feed the da Silvas for a month. José da Silva seemed astounded when I handed him two hundred dollars' worth of cruzeiros. It amounted to a year's work. Gallo and I didn't say much to one another as we drove toward my hotel. The story was finished, and this would be my final night in Rio. Flavio would die as the doctor predicted. His family would sink deeper into the mire of that stinking mountainside. Packing, I tried believing that he was simply the weapon to expose poverty in Latin America. He was much more — a boy endowed with an unselfishness that few human beings possess. Through him I witnessed more courage than I have from any other experience.

April 10, 1961

This morning I went with Gallo to say good-bye to Flavio. We met at the bottom of the favela, where he had come for more water. "Well, I leave tonight, Flav."

"When do you come back, Gorduun?"

"Oh — someday soon," I lied.

Holding my hand, he walked to the car with us. "Come back!"

"I will. I will."

Smiling, he turned slowly and hobbled back toward the mountainside. I watched until I lost sight of him climbing among the shacks of Catacumba.

New York seemed like another planet when I reached there. I had done what I was sent to do, and done it well. My reasoning came up with a loose estimate: fourteen pages and possibly a cover. Flavio da Silva deserved it. But the expression on my story editor's face spelled disaster when I went to his office two weeks later. On Tim Foote's desk was the layout — one picture of Flavio lying in bed opposite a portrait of a wealthy Brazilian woman. Quickly I thumbed through. There were no other pictures of Flavio or his family. I stared at Tim. "That's it?"

He shrugged and shook his head. "I'm afraid so. The top brass feels that such poverty isn't an appealing subject for a magazine fighting for survival against television." I went home that weekend and wrote a note to Ed Thompson, the managing editor.

Dear Ed,

I saw the Favela layout and I am shocked.

With regret I offer my resignation.

On Monday I showed the note to Tim. He, in turn, showed me a clipping from that Sunday's *New York Times*. Dean Rusk, the Secretary of State, was warning our government that if it didn't give immediate aid to the poor of Latin America, Communism would spread rapidly throughout the hemisphere. Flavio's story was in a new layout that same afternoon and scheduled for immediate publication with ten pages. I tore up the note. Flavio's story, "Freedom's Fearful Foe: Poverty," was published in the issue of June 16, 1961.

FOLLOWING The da Silva Shack in the Favela of Catacumba, Rio de Janeiro

OPPOSITE Isabel
ABOVE Albia and Isabel, the Favela

OPPOSITE Mario, Crying After Being Bitten by a Dog
ABOVE Flavio Feeding Zacarias

ABOVE Flavio Amuses Smaller Brothers and Sisters
OPPOSITE Luzia, the Favela
FOLLOWING Isabel Beside Sick Father

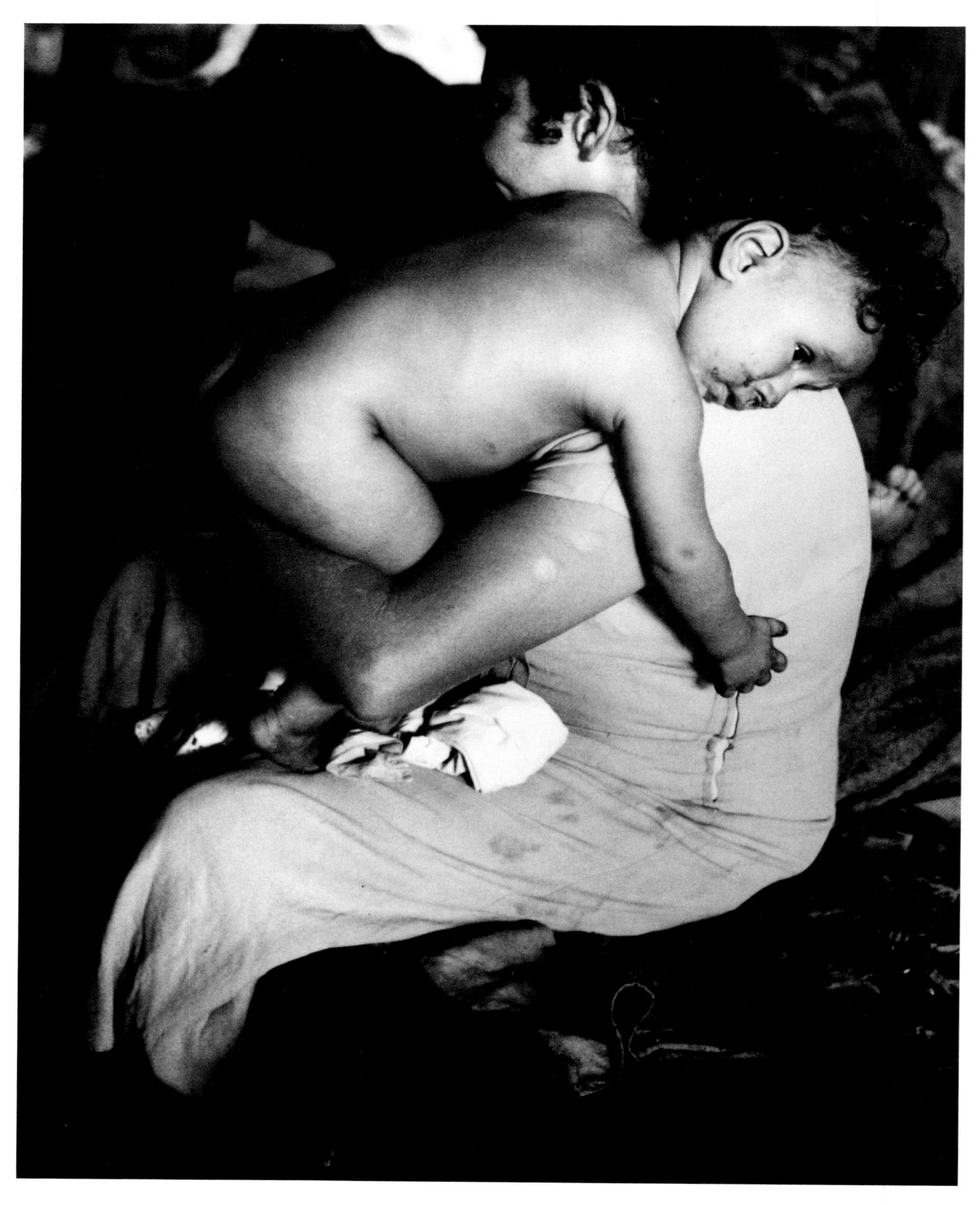

Nair da Silva and Zacarias

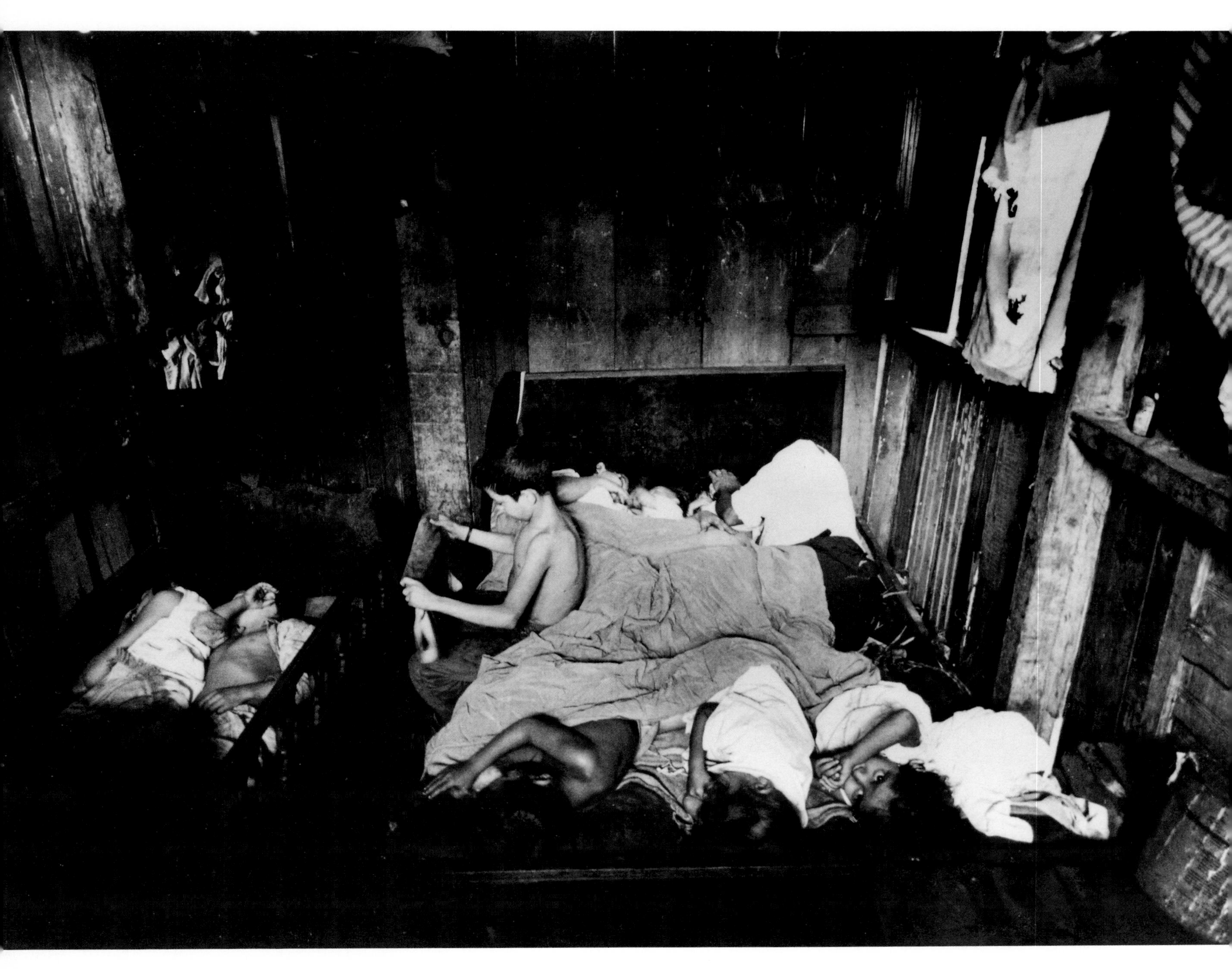

The da Silva Family at Dawn

A WEEK AFTER THE STORY WAS PUBLISHED, letters with money were pouring in. And they kept coming. Before the month was out, more than $30,000 had arrived. And with them were queries asking where food, money, and clothing could be sent. Exciting news arrived from Denver's bureau. The Children's Asthma Research Institute and Hospital in that city had volunteered to accept Flavio for treatment without charge. "We can definitely save him. Just deliver him to our door."

The decision was made. I was to go back to Rio and bring Flavio to Denver. Gallo would accompany us to act as an interpreter. But a disturbing message came from the Rio bureau: Flavio had taken a turn for the worse. What's more he was probably a tuberculosis victim. If so, there was a law prohibiting his entering our country. President Kennedy was the only one who could waive that law. He was alerted; the law was waived. Now I would be returning to this boy I had never expected to see again.

Gallo was waiting at the airport. "Flavio knows you're coming and he's excited. I found a house for the family in the Guadalupe District, several miles outside Rio. A small cottage is in the backyard that can be rented for extra income. It's a miracle." He dropped me off at my hotel, and we agreed to meet at the favela later. I changed clothes and was on my way.

The taxi dropped me across the street from the entrance to Catacumba, where a gathering of favelados milled about. "Gorduun! Gorduun!" It was Baptista, the calm da Silva child. Waving, he darted into the street to meet me. "Wait, Baptista!" I shouted. My warning came too late. A car knocked him down, passed over him, and stopped. The driver attempted to start off again, but hostile favelados surrounded the car, rocking it, screaming, "Kill him! Kill him!" Two men were trying to force open the locked doors. I lifted Baptista into my arms. He was unconscious and blood streamed from his mouth and nose.

Then Nair was running toward us. "My God! He's killed my boy!" I beat on the car door, shouting, "Hospital! Hospital!" It was the driver's chance to escape. He unlocked a back door. Nair got in, I lifted Baptista into her arms, then got in myself. The hostile favelados backed off. As we sped away Nair was rocking back and forth, wiping the blood away with her apron. The happy reunion I had hoped for had collapsed into a nightmare.

The hospital doctors were still examining Baptista behind closed doors when his father arrived with Gallo. Baptista was his favorite child. He lowered his head and prayed — and we were praying with him when we heard Baptista crying. He was alive. An hour later a doctor came out and spoke to Nair. "Your boy has a fractured collarbone and a mild head injury, but he will be all right." Baptista was finally brought out later with his shoulder in a cast, and we returned to Catacumba.

Curious, the children were inspecting Baptista's bandages when Gallo quietly broke the good news. "Your family is going to be moved into a new home far away from this favela — and there will be good food, furniture, and new clothes for everybody. Flavio is going to a hospital in America to get well."

Stunned, Nair and José da Silva stared at us in disbelief. The children exploded into joyous laughter. Flavio reached for my hand. "I'm glad you came back." Happiness was in Nair's eyes, but her husband seemed apprehensive. The day that began with disaster had been tempered with joy. But fortuitous news for the da Silvas proved otherwise for their neighbors. "Why them?" they asked. "What about us?" An unanswerable question. Their hostility was manifest. Plans to move the family had to be shortened from two weeks to one.

When Gallo and I came with a van, the da Silva family had washed up with their last tin of water. Flavio scurried about wrapping their few belongings into bundles. The neighbors had gathered to watch the departure. "I'm glad for them," Luzia's godmother said. "Maybe little Flavio will live now." Others looked on with envy. Finally we started down the mountainside, carrying all they owned in makeshift knapsacks. With Zacarias in her arms, Nair turned for a final look at the shack that had been home for twelve years, then slowly followed us down the mountainside.

Flavio trying on his new shoes
Photograph by Paulo Muniz

Word about their departure was out. A hundred or more favelados had gathered at the entrance to the favela when we reached there. The mood was tense. A few good-byes came from the crowd. One woman hugged Nair for several moments, kissed Zacarias, then went up the hill in tears. Another, with a small child, grabbed my shoulder. "All the rest of us stay here to die?" My sorrow for her was in full cry, but any answer would have been without meaning. I pulled from her grasp and we piled into the van. As we drove off, Flavio took a final glance at Catacumba. "This is the happiest day of our lives."

At the Sears, Roebuck store the entire family got new clothing, and toys were given to the children. The journey to the new home was tumultuous. The entire neighborhood had turned out to greet them. A hush fell when we pulled to a stop in front of their new home. Grasping their new belongings, they got out slowly, then began entering. José da Silva bowed to his new neighbors as they greeted him. Once inside, the family became silent. Nair shook her head. "Good Lord, this is all for us?" "All for you," Gallo answered softly.

Flavio shook his head. "Will my family really live here when I am gone?"

"It's their home forever, Flav." Then, like a dam bursting, the children ran through the house — inspecting furniture, jumping on beds, and flushing the toilet over and over again. Hesitantly, Nair walked into the kitchen. There was a new refrigerator and a gas range. The neighborhood women had unpacked and washed every plate and the silverware. *Feijoada,* a Brazilian dish of rice, beans, meat, and vegetables, simmered in a large pot on the stove. José da Silva stood in the kitchen doorway, viewing the small cottage at the edge of a paved backyard. "I just can't believe this," he whispered. By eight o'clock the neighborhood women had fed them, cleaned up the kitchen, and gone. Flavio went to say good-bye to the smaller ones after they got into their beds. He wouldn't see them again for two years.

Our plane would leave for New York at midnight. Maria, having put on her new nightgown, watched as Flavio packed. For a moment, they faced each other rather awkwardly. Then giggling, she hurried to her room. Neither said good-bye.

Nair had avoided Flavio most of the day. When it was time for him to leave he went to touch her arm. "Good-bye, Momma." She remained silent, looking toward the wall. He touched her again. "I have to go now, Momma."

Suddenly she turned and enclosed him in her arms, sobbing. "God will protect you, son. Go now." Quickly, he took my hand and pulled me toward the door.

José da Silva was waiting in the car hired to take us to the airport. "You're sure they won't kick us out next week and take all this stuff back?" he asked. "It's yours, José. Our office will find you a job somewhere and a truck to help you earn a living."

By now the media had made that son the most celebrated twelve-year-old in the Western Hemisphere. An array of floodlights, newsmen, and television cameras met us at the terminal. When the curious closed in for a look at Flavio, the overpowering events of the week suddenly caught up with him. Ducking beneath my arm, he began to weep. José da Silva touched his head tenderly — probably for the first time in years. "Be a good boy" was all he could bring himself to say. Varig Airline's officials rushed us to our plane. Later, as it moved forward for takeoff, we could see José da Silva watching from the edge of the airstrip. Gallo shook his head. "That poor guy still can't believe what's happening to him."

Once inside the first-class cabin, Flavio composed himself and settled into his seat. His hand reached for mine as the airliner streaked down the runway. When it roared upward, his nails dug into my palms. The "big bird" he had longed to fly on banked and leveled off, carrying him toward New York. A stewardess brought him chocolates and a small model of the plane in which he was flying. A sumptuous dinner was served, but he was too excited to eat. After the cabin lights dimmed he fell asleep. I looked at him. Whatever he dreamt couldn't possibly have prefigured the life he was about to begin.

Our stopover in New York was cut short. Flavio fainted in the hotel hallway, so we decided to rush him to Denver. There was another problem. Flavio refused to take off his new shoes — even in bed. He was afraid they would be stolen. At Denver, photographers and people from the Institute were waiting. When the flashbulbs started popping, Flavio took refuge under my arm again, and we were whisked away from the confusion.

On July 7, 1961, Flavio was put into the hands of the people who promised to save him. Dr. Falliers, the head of Flavio's medical team, asked him to undress. He removed all his clothing except his shoes. "Come on, Flav. Take off the shoes," Gallo pleaded.

"No! No! Somebody will steal them!" Finally Gallo and I had to hold him down. When a doctor pulled off one shoe, Flavio shrieked. The foot was covered with pus and blisters. The doctors decided to cut the other shoe off. His tears cascaded when he saw his beautiful shoe cut to pieces. When I promised him another pair exactly like them, the tears subsided. In new sneakers, a couple of hours later, he was pumping wildly on a playground swing, surrounded by admiring boys and girls. Gallo would stay on for two weeks to quell the uneasiness Flavio was sure to experience.

Before leaving for the airport I took Flavio aside. "The doctors who cut up your shoe didn't want to hurt you." He nodded as though he understood. As my taxi pulled away

Flavio, emotionally spent, with author at Rio de Janeiro airport en route to New York
Photograph by Paulo Muniz

I watched him until he reentered the gate of his new home. On the plane I read a note Dr. Falliers had given me: "Flavio's enlarged chest cavity confirms suspicion that he has one of the severest types of asthma. X rays indicate that at twelve he has the bone structure of a boy nine. His weight and height are those of a six-year-old."

The July cover of *Life* portrayed Flavio da Silva smiling his thanks to those who were trying to save him. But those pages made it clear that in molding human lives, money alone could not finish what it had begun. The da Silvas would have to build on their miracle, and not lapse into dependency. A smiling Flavio did not solve the problems he dramatized. He was one of a numberless multitude, a symbol through which one might understand the tragedy of poverty.

Flavio's two-year sojourn at the Institute was a godsend. Once a frail, sickly child, he grew to be a healthy boy, suffering only one more serious attack. But he had to learn to cope with his problems during those two years. Taking strong medication, studying English, and adjusting to the discipline of a new way of life were, at times, misery. When it was time for his departure there was sadness — for those who had grown to love him, and for him as well. Resigned to leaving, he sent his clothes to be cleaned, wrote notes to his friends, and bought gifts for his entire family.

Perhaps my hopes for Flavio da Silva were always beyond his reach. He was past the peak for learning certain academic skills when he arrived at Denver. He would be returning to something radically different. Surely he couldn't compete with the average Brazilian child his age. His future remained unpromising. The early corrosive illness, the ruinous deprivation had taken their toll.

He was discharged from the Institute on July 27, 1963. Ruth Fowler, from *Life*'s publisher's office, went to escort him to New York. During his final moments he sat in his room feeling abandoned. When she found him staring out the window, he wiped away tears, smiled, and said, "Okay, Ruth — let's go." His friends helped carry his bags to the waiting car. He got into it, then waved a final good-bye.

Flavio stayed in New York for forty-eight hours before flying on to Brazil. Virginia Hansen was to accompany him back to Rio. I had flown in from Paris to be with him for a day. My plans for lunch at a good restaurant were thwarted. He insisted on hot dogs, a Coke, and ice cream. At the airport the next morning, he took me aside. "Gordon, I don't want to go back to Brazil. Can't you keep me here like I was your son?"

"I'd love to keep you, Flav. But your father wouldn't allow it. Right now it's impossible. Well, maybe . . ." I stopped. It was no time for a lie. I, his last hope, had failed him. After a short silence, he said, "It's not that I don't want to see my family. I love them, but I also like it here in America. I could do much better here and someday I'll send for all of them. Understand?"

"We'll see, Flav. We'll see." His flight was called, and reluctantly he went down the ramp. In the blur of passengers, I lost sight of him — hoping he wouldn't keep chasing a fu-

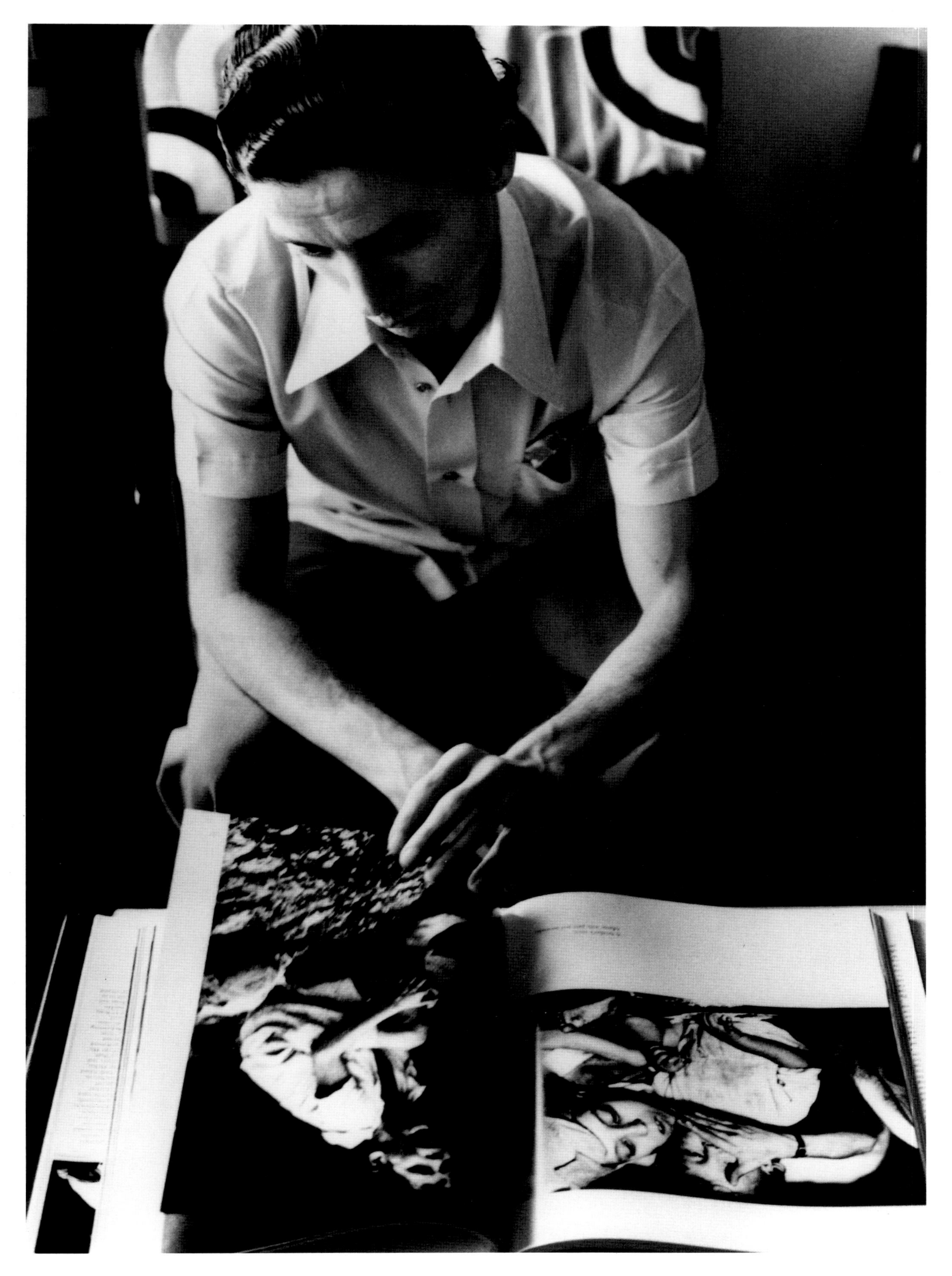

Flavio Looking at the *Life* Story, 1977

tile dream. Yet who was to know? His miracle had already convinced me that no space was larger than that of hope.

Ten years later I went back to Brazil to see Flavio. Now, he was in the house he had bought for his wife, Cleuza, and their two sons, Flavio Jr. and Felipe Luiz. That house, sitting on a "real street," had pots, pans, and three beds with clean sheets. His employer, a wealthy Brazilian with a mansion outside Rio, feared that his son might be kidnapped. Flavio, armed with a pistol, had been hired to prevent that.

Things at his parents' house were not good. His father was living far away and only came to take Nair's wash money. A sadness swept over him when he told me this. We dropped the subject. On the final afternoon of my three-day visit, we sat in my hotel room eating hamburgers. He picked up the old *Life* magazine I had brought and turned to the picture of himself lying ill on the bed. "I was going to die if you had not come."

"Maybe not, Flav."

"Oh, yes, I knew. I still worry about my brothers and sisters, but I've got my own family now, and I must look after them." He turned to a page showing that shack perched high on the side of Catacumba. "The favela's gone. They tore it down after your story, but my father's house is like that again." He stood up to leave, took a small package from his pocket, and handed it to me. "This is from Cleuza and me. Open it on the plane. We'll be at the airport tonight."

Other difficult farewells to Flavio had prompted my plan to simply say, "Well, so long, Flav," and then leave as quickly as possible. It didn't happen that way. When my flight was called he pulled me aside and spoke softly. "Every day I still think about taking my family to America, Gordon. I want a job there, and I want my wife and children to see the young friends I knew back in Denver. Please — see if you can help us."

I wanted to say, "Flav, most of those young friends are dead. They were beyond saving." I actually said, "I'll try, Flav." I left him once again, not daring to hope for another miracle. The one that had taken place on Catacumba belonged to the past. On the plane I opened the package he had given me that afternoon. Inside was a handsome black billfold, pictures of Felipe and Flavio Jr., and a note saying, "Happy Father's Day, Gordon. We love you." Somewhere, down there on the road to Guadalupe was Flavio, still with his dreams.

Thirty-five years have gone by. Forty-seven now, kicked off his job, Flavio is again suffering the pains of poverty. His severance pay for thirteen years' work — $400. Separated from Clueza for more than six years, he lives, with sixteen others, in the house that *Life*'s readers bought — a house that crumbles from neglect. José da Silva is confined to a mental institution. No longer does he remember his children's names. The hopes of his oldest child seem to have come to an end — his fondest dreams chewed up without good reason. I won't forsake Flavio da Silva in his present predicament. It places me at his side once more.

Flavio During Author's Second Visit to Brazil, 1977

Fontenelle Family

THE OUTCOME OF YET ANOTHER ESSAY about poverty leaves me wondering about the problem of altering human lives. Norman Fontenelle Sr. and his wife, Bessie, lived in a rotting Harlem tenement building across the world from the Da Silvas, but, with nine children, they shared the same kind of impoverishment. I became involved in their struggle in 1967 after Philip Kunhardt, *Life*'s managing editor at the time, asked me why black people were rioting and why they were so discontented, especially in the big cities. In a short search for a black family whose plight would give the answer, I had found the Fontenelles, hungry and falling apart. Winter was coming on, and it was a bad time for them. These were the first words Norman Fontenelle spoke to me: "There's hardly enough food in our icebox to fill the baby's stomach."

For nearly a week I had visited the family daily without using my camera. I wanted to become a part of them first. When I reached their place one morning Bessie lay crying with Richard, the youngest child, under her arm. "Why are you weeping?" I asked.

She answered simply, "I sent Norman to the hospital last night."

"Why? What's wrong with him?"

"Well, he's all frustrated, without a job. He kicked little Norman out in the cold last night and then beat up on me. I couldn't take any more. After he went to sleep I boiled a cauldron of wash water, poured in some honey, and dumped it on him." She wiped at the tears. "All this needing and wanting is just about to drive my whole family crazy."

"Why the honey?"

"To make it stick."

Bessie's family was my answer to Philip Kunhardt's question about black discontent. My opening block of text, along with the pictures, expressed that discontent to America — most of which still hangs on: What I am, what you force me to be, is what you are. For I am you staring back from a mirror of poverty and despair, of revolt and freedom. Look at me and know that to destroy me is to destroy yourself. You are weary of the long hot summers. I am tired of the long hungered winters. We are not so far apart as it might seem. There is something about both of us that goes deeper than blood or black and white. It is our common search for a better life, a better world, I march over the same ground you once marched. I fight for the same things you still fight for. My needs are the same as your children's. I too am America. America is me. It gave me the only life I know — so I must share in its survival. Look at me. Listen to me. Try to understand my struggle against your racism. There is yet a chance to live in peace beneath these restless skies.

The story was published in 1968. Letters and money came in. With funds *Life* magazine contributed, a small house with new furnishings was bought for the Fontenelles on Long Island. There were grass, fresh air, and schools nearby for the children. A job was found for Norman Sr. Fate, it now seemed, had lifted them from the filth and chaos of that awful Harlem tenement.

But three months later, at three o'clock one morning, Norman Sr. came in drunk and

At the Poverty Board: Bessie and Kenneth, Little Richard, Norman Jr., and Ellen

dropped a lit cigarette onto the new sofa. In the flames that followed, he and Kenneth, his small son, died. The others escaped, but the house was completely destroyed. Bessie Fontenelle, the distraught widow, fled back to Harlem.

Several years had passed when I went to visit her on a Christmas Eve. The family was scattered. Two sons were in prison, one for drug peddling; the other for smashing a store window and taking a small radio. Three of her teenage daughters were, in her words, "on the streets." Only she and Richard, the child she still had hope for, remained in the cramped, cold quarters. I gave her money I had brought. As I left she stood at the top of the stairs, saying finally what I couldn't bring myself to say, "Merry Christmas." Weakly, I called back, "A Happier New Year."

Disaster kept finishing off the Fontenelle children one by one. I attended Roseanna's funeral; she had died from a hole in her heart and drugs. Bessie Fontenelle sat near the cheap coffin frozen in grief. Her family was dwindling away.

Years later, on the first day of 1990, I went to visit Bessie Fontenelle again. She was alone. By now, Richard was married and had a child named Gordon. "Richard's going to do all right. Doesn't drink or smoke. Maybe one of my kids will make it before I'm gone." She sighed. "The others are lost. Norman Jr.'s back in prison. Riel died from an overdose and Ellen's sick with AIDS. Her baby's already dead from the same thing. I've got diabetes, and cancer's chewing me up. Guess I'm dying too."

Rosie Cleaning the Bathtub

Two months later Bessie Fontenelle did die. Huddled together against a cold March wind, Richard, Diana, Lette, and Ellen watched silently as she was lowered into the frozen earth already covering Kenneth, Riel, Roseanna, and their father. Norman Jr. grieved from prison. Harry was somewhere out of reach in Ohio, ducking drug pushers he owed. Not long after, death from AIDS claimed both Lette and Ellen.

Recently Richard called to wish me a happy Father's Day. "How's everything?" I asked.

"Not good. My oldest sister Diana's on a drug cure up in the Bronx."

"And Norman Junior?"

"Forgot to tell you. He died a couple of weeks ago. Don't know what he died from." Most of his family was gone.

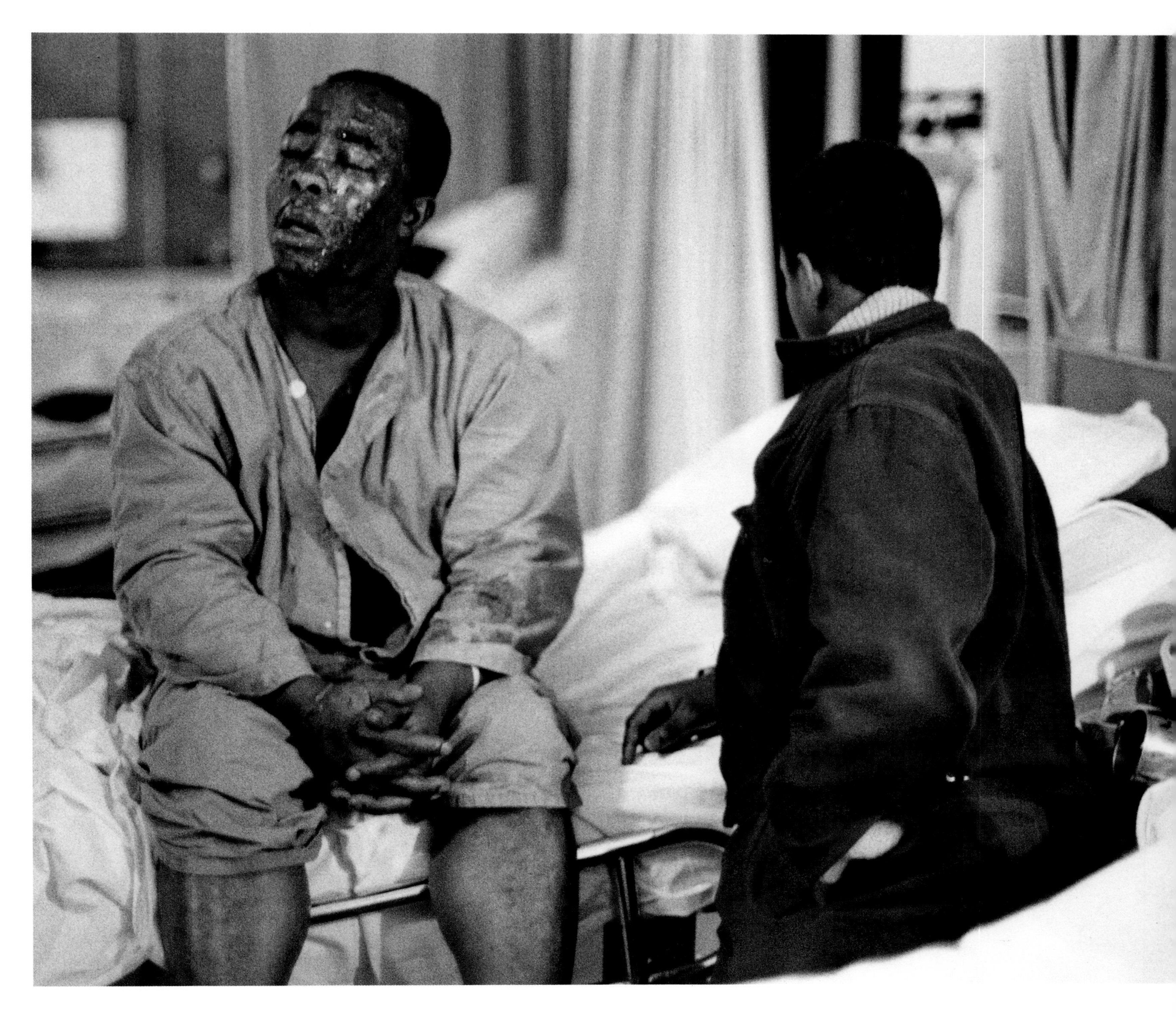

Norman Sr., Burned from Scalding, Is Visited by Norman Jr. at Hospital

DUK

OPPOSITE Fontenelle Children Outside Their Harlem Tenement
BELOW Norman Jr. Reading in Bed

ABOVE Norman Sr.
OPPOSITE Ellen, Crying

BELOW Ellen's Feet
OPPOSITE The Only Picture Hanging in the Fontenelle Home in Harlem

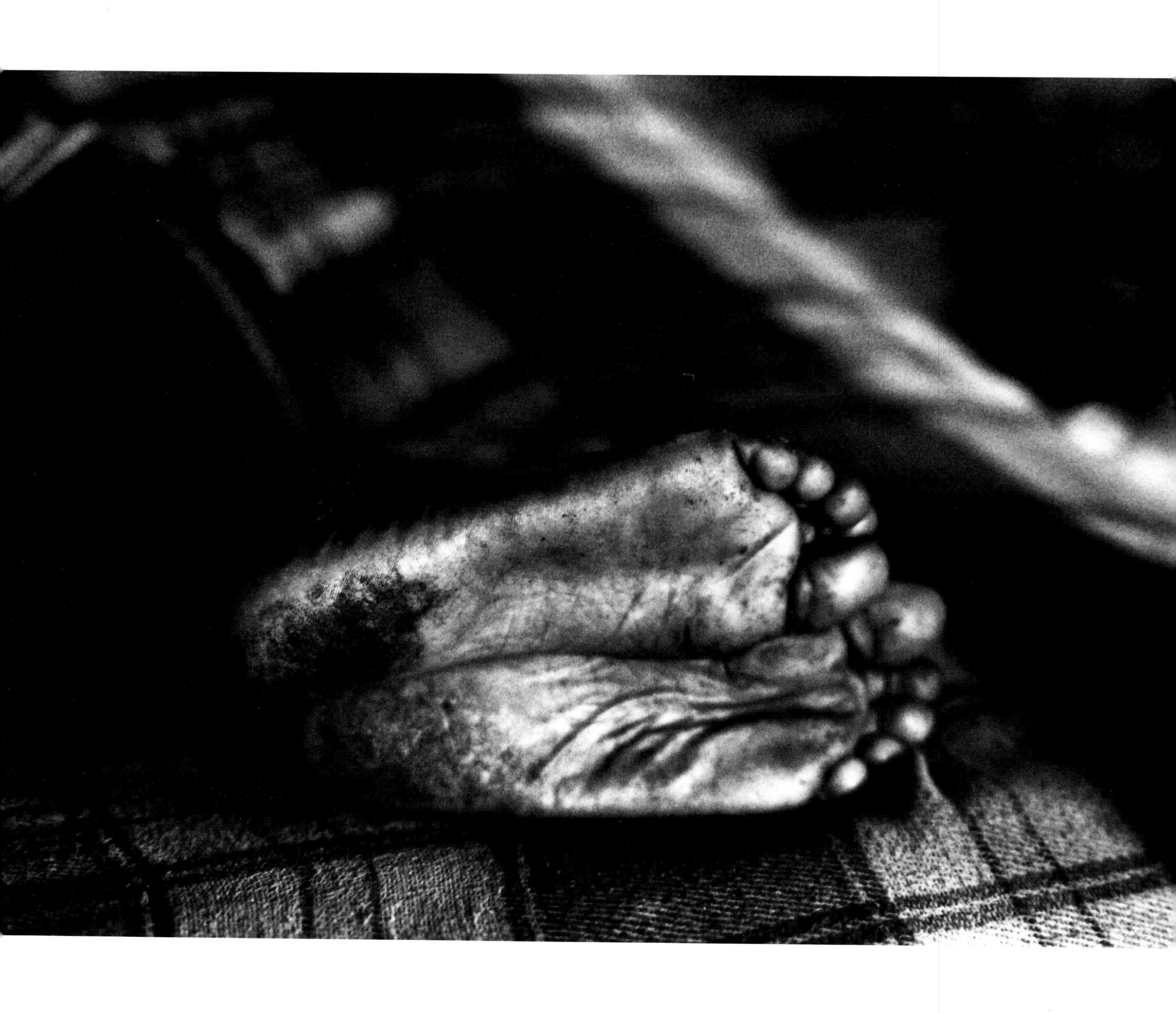

FOLLOWING Bessie and Little Richard the Morning After She Scalded Her Husband

BELOW Black Muslim Rally, New York, 1963
OPPOSITE Malcolm X Addressing Black Muslim Rally in Chicago, 1963

Civil Rights

IN 1963 THE TURBULENT BLACK REVOLUTION was steadily building and *Life* magazine wanted to cover it. The Muslims and Malcolm X, their fiery spokesman, had become the magazine's first target. Other forces were slowly gathering — the Black Panthers, Huey Newton, Stokely Carmichael, Eldridge Cleaver, and Bobby Seales would come later to stridently berate racism throughout the nation. Infiltration into their volatile camps by a white publication that was held suspect seemed impossible. Whatever attempts the magazine had made had fallen flat. It seems reasonable that at the time, *Life*'s editors would question my ability to report objectively about black militancy. I was black and my sentiments lay in the heart of black fury sweeping the country.

Certainly the black militants would have their doubts about me as well. I was a black member of a white team. But they wanted to be heard, and I was in a position to accommodate them through the pages of a prestigious magazine. Bluntly, the editors put the question to me: "Do you think you can cover the Black Muslims with a white reporter?"

"No."

"How about a black reporter?"

"I doubt that they will accept me. If they do I would have to write my own story."

"Okay. Give it a try."

The following afternoon I went up to a corner on Harlem's 125th Street and Seventh Avenue, where Malcolm X was addressing a huge crowd. With controlled rage he was spewing anger at the white cops sitting astride their horses. "You're no better than the pimps, hustlers, and dope peddlers up here! You're worse! I'm telling you like it is! We Muslims defy you pale-face devils. Touch a Muslim and may God have mercy on your souls!" He went on for an hour. The cops looked straight ahead, some with folded arms, some calmly stroking their chins with anger in their eyes.

I followed Malcolm to the Muslim Restaurant on Lenox Avenue and introduced myself. "I know who you are," he said. "Come have some tea." Over our second cup I presented my problem. "I want to cover the Nation of Islam for *Life* magazine."

He smiled. "So do a lot of people." After a short silence he said, "Permission would have to be granted by the Messenger, the honorable Elijah Muhammad, and he's out in Arizona."

"Would you fly out there with me to see him?"

"Yes. I could manage that."

Elijah Muhammad, a small, gentle-appearing man, entered the living room where we awaited him. After an embrace from Malcolm he turned on me with a stern look. "Why does a bright young man like you work for white devils?" Taken aback I gave an answer that alluded to being inside a Trojan horse, where I could keep an eye on the enemy. He didn't buy that. Within thirty minutes Malcolm and I were headed back toward the airport without an answer.

"I think he likes you," Malcolm said as we drove along.

"If he does, he's got a poor way of showing it."

Malcolm laughed. "I think he'll invite you back."

Elijah did invite me back two weeks later, and staring at me he said, "I'll give you five hundred thousand dollars to do a motion picture and a book on the Nation of Islam. How about it?"

My answer was no less calculated than his offer. "Sir, I am honored and flattered, but I'm afraid that you might try to wield some influence over me."

He smiled for the first time. "If I put that much money in your pockets, I would indeed influence you."

"So — I have to refuse."

Malcolm and I were leaving when he called me back. "Young man, I like the fact that you turned down a half million dollars on your principles." He thought for a moment. "I'm going to let you do a story on the Nation of Islam. Brother Malcolm will be your guide. If I like it, you'll get a big box of cigars. If I don't, we'll be out to visit you."

The Messenger had given me his blessing, and my journey through the Nation was thorough. I was welcome at all rituals, even at ones where one was taught to kill "in self-defense." I came to like and respect Malcolm and address him as "brother." He seemed to like me, but from him it was always "Mr. Parks." I was beside him on the night the Los Angeles police entered the Muslims' mosque, shot it up, and killed a member. I remained close by him when the Muslims were put on trial later on. We were aboard a late flight to New York. "Brother," he said, "my daughter Qubilah needs a godfather and I nominate you. How about it?"

Shocked, I answered, "I'd be honored." A few minutes later he was snoring with his head against my shoulder. As he left our taxi in New York the next morning, I stopped him. "Malcolm, you called me brother for the first time last night."

He smiled. "You finally earned it. See you later."

Elijah Muhammad, Arizona, 1963

I was assigned to write the story about his death. The day after it was published the FBI informed the magazine that I had been targeted. *Life*'s editors did what they thought was best. A day later I was on a plane with my wife, Elizabeth, my children, Gordon Jr. and his wife, Toni and her husband, and David, along with my grandson, Alain — out over the Atlantic flying to safety. When, after a month, I came back alone to face the threat, *Life* put me up in a suite at the Hotel Plaza — surrounded with five detectives. Wearied after weeks of forced seclusion I finally slipped away from my protection and went to the Muslim Restaurant in Harlem where Malcolm and I had met. There I had tea with Brother Joseph, the head of the Muslim security force. We parted with a handshake. No mention was made of Malcolm or the reason for my visit. Later that day I dismissed the detectives and sent for my family. *Life,* not thoroughly convinced of my safety, sent a squad of police with me to welcome them. That box of cigars the Messenger promised never arrived.

OPPOSITE Newsman Being Frisked at Muslim Rally in Chicago, 1963
THIS PAGE FROM TOP
Muslim Training Against Police Dogs, Chicago, 1963;
Harlem Rally, New York, 1963;
Muslim Training for Self-defense, Chicago, 1963

ABOVE Evening Prayer, Muslim Father and Son, New York, 1963
LEFT Black Muslim Schoolchildren in Chicago, 1963

Ethel Shariff in Chicago, 1963

MOST OF US, unsure of what we can do, withdraw from things that might unveil possibilities, and those possibilities then go unrealized. An important incident that affected my career bears this out. Carl Mydans, *Life*'s eloquent writer and photographer, had a sincere interest in my Kansas childhood, and he often urged me to talk about it. One Friday as we were leaving the office, he said, "You've got a good novel inside you. Why don't you write it?"

I chuckled. "I can't write a novel."

"Did you ever try?"

"Nope."

"Give it some thought this weekend — then try."

The following Monday I handed him seven double-spaced pages that opened with a cyclone swirling over my hometown in Kansas. The title was *The Learning Tree*. He scanned it rather casually. "I want to show this to somebody." Two days later I got a phone call.

"This is Evan Thomas. I'm a friend of Carl Mydans, and I'd like to have lunch with you this Thursday."

"That's fine with me." Puzzled, I went to Carl. "Who is Evan Thomas? He invited me to lunch."

Carl smiled. "He's only the executive vice president of Harper and Row Publishing Company." He thought for a moment. "I'd better go to lunch with you."

"Right," I said, "you'd better come along."

Evan staggered me as we checked our wraps at Michael's Pub. "We want your novel. We can only advance you five thousand dollars since it will be your first book." Carl and I traded looks and kept our silence. Halfway to our table Evan stopped for a moment. "We might consider seven thousand five hundred. How does that sound?" I could only pretend that I was thinking it over. We were seated when he took off his glasses and wiped them. "Ten thousand dollars. That's as high as we can go."

"Mr. Thomas," I replied, "I may not be able to write another decent paragraph — but since you offered me all that money I'm damned well going to try." One year later, in 1963, *The Learning Tree* was published in six languages as the Harper Find of the Year.

Based on an excerpt from *The Learning Tree:*

CHRISTMAS AT SPIT'S REFORM SCHOOL FOR BOYS wasn't much different from any other day. A few of the well-behaved had been granted trips home for the holidays. The others got bean soup, a pork chop, and a small bag of peppermint candies. Marcus Savage, like four others on the top cell floor, lay alone. A card signed by Newt, Beansy, Jappy, Earl, and Skunk lay on the table beside his cot. He glanced at the names, remembering their faces as they stood against him on the road near the river. It was Newt, he felt, who had betrayed him. Then white faces came smirking at him — Kirky, that peckerwood cop, and that redneck Judge Cavaugh. He began boiling inside. With a vicious swipe he sent the card sailing across the floor. It would be May before he would see Cherokee Flats again.

He had settled back on the cot when Crapper, the guard, hollered through the bars at him. "You got some visitors, Savage! Git your black ass up and try lookin' happy!"

"Screw you!"

"Fool with me and you don't see nobody!"

"I don't give a goddam. Ain't nobody I want to see nohow." But by now the visitors were coming down the corridor.

"Right this way, Rev'rend." Crapper spoke with a false politeness. The cell door remained shut to Reverend Broadnap, Maggie Pullens, and Deacon Fuller.

Marcus's body stiffened as Broadnap began to speak. "We have come to wish you a Merry Christmas, son." Remaining on his cot, Marcus looked up at him with a frown. Broadnap knelt and motioned the others to their knees. "Let's pray." Marcus kept his eyes lowered.

"O Almighty God, we come to you on bended knee prayin' for the soul of this young sinner." Marcus's eyes shot defiantly to Crapper, who stood with a grin on his face. "Wash his sins away with the white snow of Christmas. Lighten his darkness. Bring peace to his troubled soul. Help him to leave this place a better young man. O God, show him the light. Show —"

"Shut up! Shut up!" Marcus was up on his feet shouting. "Git the hell outta here! I don't wanta hear none of your damn Uncle Tom prayin' over me!"

Shocked, the three visitors rose. "You don't know what you're sayin', son," Broadnap whispered.

Marcus spit on the floor. "I know as much about what I'm sayin' as you do!"

Broadnap took out a card. A picture of Christ was on it and he placed it on the floor inside the bars. "Read the scripture there on the back, son. Pray to the Savior. He'll hear you."

Marcus snatched up the card and threw it at the preacher. "You and your white-trash God can git the hell outta here! I don't want no part of you soul savers or your white God!" Tears were in his eyes. "Look at Crapper there! He's white! Whyn't you git down and moan to him so he can kick the crap outta you like he does to us nigga' boys. Yeh, that's what he calls us — nigga'! nigga'! nigga'! Tell 'em Crapper. Tell 'em what you gonna do to me when they're gone! Tell 'em!"

"Son —"

"Don't 'son' me. Just git goin'! Then Crapper can tease me 'bout you nigga's comin' here to pray over me!"

They filed out silently as Crapper followed them down the corridor. Marcus sat thinking for a while. A sense of guilt was taking over. They had come to help him, and he had sent them away hurt. His anger was meant for Crapper's ears, not theirs. It was that grin on Crapper's face that had brought it on. It was too late now; the harm was done. Crapper came back, picked up the card, pulled out a pencil, blackened the face of Jesus, and flung it back into the cell. The grin had widened. "Merry Christmas — nigga'. Now you've got a black God."

Marcus remained silent as his head fell back into the shadows. He closed his eyes, trying to form the image of a God with black skin. He couldn't. That pale saintly image with blue eyes had been implanted in his mind too long. He picked up the card, tore it in half, and threw it back through the bars.

Genevieve Young, my editor, had patiently nursed me through my first bestseller. Today *The Learning Tree* is still on bookstore shelves and in classrooms around the country and is approaching its sixtieth printing. A year later Genevieve pulled me through another autobiographical work, *A Choice of Weapons*. Carl Mydans had nudged me into another career. Soon I was knee deep in the problems of writing, with no realization that seventeen other books were to follow.

IN THE MIDST OF THIS TIME OF UNREST in America, I recall a sudden trip overseas for *Life*. It was in January of 1965, when death was closing in on Winston Churchill. Having been sent to London three weeks earlier to await its arrival, I was beginning to feel somewhat ghoulish. "Well, how is Sir Winston doing?" I asked the hotel concierge one morning.

"Oh — the old boy's hanging on. A tough one, you know. He won't go easy."

When finally time ran out on England's prime minister, the elaborate plans for his funeral were already set. Now, on this cold winter morning, they were explicit. The cortege amounted to a striking homage to the hero. Thousands lined the route of a procession that seemed endless. Alongside scores of other photographers, I trained my camera's sight on the sea of marchers accompanying the coffin. Colorfully bedecked in every military uniform of the British Empire, they moved slowly toward the cathedral. (See pages 160 and 161.)

Life's preparedness for the occasion went unchallenged. A huge jet aircraft — refurbished with film-processing laboratories and facilities for the managing editor and staff — sat at Heathrow Airport, waiting for the takes of the photographers assigned to the event. Messengers on motorcycles arrived in shifts to rush our film to the plane. Churchill was still being eulogized as the huge jet streaked down the runway — racing against time and the competitiveness of television. Before the jet set down in Chicago, the story would be ready for the presses.

MY FIRST NOVEL had spread its shadow westward. John Cassavetes, the actor, called one night from Hollywood. "I've just finished *The Learning Tree*. It should be made into a motion picture; and you should direct it."

I laughed. "Thanks, John, but you know there are no black directors in Hollywood — and I'm afraid there won't be any."

"Can you get out here by day after tomorrow?"

"That's possible."

"Okay. Come to Warner Brothers Studio in Burbank around four o'clock. I'll be waiting in Kenny Hyman's office. His old man owns the joint."

After my arrival Cassavetes introduced me to Hyman and left abruptly. Later I was to learn that they were so angry with one another they were hardly speaking. Kenny's first words stunned me: "I've just read your book, and the studio is ready to make a film of it under your direction." Doubt was in my eyes — and he recognized it. "I'm dead serious," he said.

"Fine," I answered, but disbelief still wavered through me.

"Who would you like to write the screenplay?"

"I don't know anyone out here."

"Why don't you write it yourself? You wrote the book."

"Okay."

"Cassavetes tells me you're a composer as well. You might as well do the score."

"Fine by me."

"Good. Now, since you'll be Hollywood's first black director, you'll need some clout. I suggest you produce it for the studio as well."

"Why not?" I returned to New York still feeling that I was a recipient of Hollywood double-talk. But a few weeks later I moved into Warner Brothers Studio and began the overwhelming task of directing my first feature film. My screenplay was accepted on the first draft. Sure of myself now, I left *Life* magazine. From then on I would work for it only on a contractual basis.

Three months later, actors, crew members, and trucks of equipment were arriving on location in my hometown—in the novel, Cherokee Flats. As we approached the first morning of shooting I sat next to Burney Guffey, my wizened cameraman. My hands were constantly rubbing together, showing my nervousness. Burney smiled. "Everything's gonna be fine."

Author directs *The Learning Tree*
Photograph by Gordon Parks Jr.

While the technicians made final preparations, I took Kyle Johnson aside and spoke to him. "From this moment on, you're Newt Winger. I lived him, wrote about him, and now I'm turning him over to you."

Kyle, a sensitive young man of seventeen, smiled and patted my shoulder. "I'll do my best."

The moment had arrived. I went to the huge crane and took my seat beside the camera operator. Smoothly it lifted us high into the air. Beyond were the rolling green plains where I had spent the first fifteen years of my life. Now, with millions of dollars behind me, I had come back to relive a distant past. Just a few miles westward, Momma and Poppa lay side by side in segregated graves, and I longed for their presence. The cameras focused on Kyle. He was ready. I signaled to my assistant. "Cameras," he said softly.

"Cameras rolling," Burney answered.

"Action!" The word spurted out of me like a flame. And squinting against the sun, Kyle started moving over what was once my father's cornfield. *The Learning Tree* was on its way.

Trauma was plentiful throughout the three months of filming. Kyle came to my room one night troubled by a scene he was to enact the following morning. "How did you really feel when you slept by your mother's coffin that night?" he asked.

"Sad. Frightened." I reached for the book and turned to a page. "Read this passage before you go to sleep. It might help." That passage concerned a desperate attempt to abolish my fear of death:

> Newt pushed the door open, paused, then stepped into the room. In the dimness he could see the shape of his mother's coffin. Slowly he moved toward it with sweat dripping from his armpits. Then gently he lifted the lid and looked. His mother lay deep in the cushion of crinkled white. He took a final look, dropped the blanket to the floor. Then lying upon it, he pulled it around his shoulders, closed his eyes tightly, and began the struggle with sleep.

The next morning Kyle emerged from the scene in tears. He was not alone; toughened crew members wiped at their eyes as well. For safety, I wanted to shoot the scene twice, but I couldn't bring myself to ask it of him. I glanced at Guffey. "How was the camera? Are you happy?" His thumbs pointed upward.

The following week the governor of Kansas proclaimed a day in my honor — and he came from Topeka for the celebration. I expressed my thanks, as well as disdain for the segregated graveyard where Momma and Poppa lay together. Two days later a gentleman arrived from the mayor's office. "His Honor wants to move your mother's remains to the white side. He hopes you will agree to that."

"No — I don't agree. Tell His Honor that the road leading to the black graves needs paving, and that weeds there are higher than the tombstones. I find segregated graves to be intolerable. Never will I lie in one."

Another six months of exhausting work would pass before *The Learning Tree* premiered on Broadway. Several years later the Library of Congress's James Billington would select it for the National Film Registry. Carl Mydans, John Cassavetes, Kenneth Hyman, a fine cast, and a dedicated crew had made it possible. Genevieve Young, my editor at Harper and Row, having brought in the sun and moon, had also brought in an irresistible love. Eventually, after a painful divorce from Elizabeth, she and I took our marriage vows.

Gene Young Parks, author's third wife

ON APRIL 4, 1968, I WAS IN CALIFORNIA. Philip Kunhardt, *Life*'s managing editor, called.

"Well — you know what happened."

"It's terrible."

"Can you go to Atlanta for the funeral?"

"I'll take the first plane out."

"Fine. Write what you feel."

"I'll do that."

Without any murmurings of doubt, *Life* printed what I wrote, and I share here the heart of it:

> Martin Luther King lay in his coffin — murdered by a white assassin's bullet. Packed to the walls, Atlanta's Ebenezer Baptist Church was carrying me back to the funerals of my childhood. Here again, the stench of carnations sweetening the Southern closeness; the robed choir singing hymns familiar to our down-home Sabbath; the minister and elders praying for God to take in the departed soul; the widow, heavily veiled in grief; her tearful children; the black congregation — strangely mixed with a few white faces, mourning the loss.
>
> But something hauntingly different was echoing through Ebenezer — the scratchy, taped voice of the man we sorrowed for, ". . . and if you're around when I have to meet my day, I don't want a long funeral. And if you get somebody to deliver the eulogy, tell him not to talk too long." The revivalist voice rolled on. "I'd like somebody to mention that day that Martin Luther King, Jr., tried to love somebody. . . ." I kept remembering back, through the smell of camphor and swishing fans. Things hadn't got that much better. Our most revered spokesman would soon lie in a black burial ground. "I want you to be able to say that day that I did try to feed the hungry. I want you to say that I tried to love and serve humanity!"
>
> In death lay the man who had filled us with a hope that seemed, at this despairing moment, shattered. But in death he had made us know who we were, and that we were still in a land of oppression.
>
> How really moved is the white conscience? Racists warned Dr. King that they would kill him. They kept their word. Now, the air in dozens of American cities is darkening to arsonist smoke — the black ghetto's answer to the deed. Over a Mississippi bonfire Martin had shouted: "I'm tired of shooting, clubs, killing, and war! I won't resort to violence! Love is the only weapon!" He was preaching love when the white man sent a bullet through his neck. We struggle to distinguish between *this* act and *white* conscience.
>
> That all whites shouldn't be blamed for what one did is not enough any-

more. We are angry. You have pushed us to the edge of the precipice. Burning and looting won't help, but how else could you expect the black man to express his frustration? Should he have called the white cop, the white mayor, or the White House? Where is the killer? What will the law do with him if he is caught? Black people are demanding answers, and America must demonstrate the integrity of its conscience before we realize the worth of any answer.

We have grown to doubt your promises, and the hopeful songs of our fathers. No man spoke harder against violence. He led us into fire hoses, police clubs and dogs with his only armor, truth; his weapon, love. Now he lies dead. Martin said, "A man must conquer the fear of death, otherwise he is lost already." Fires still burn furiously, and extremists are buying guns. Army troops stand ready. Our President is warned against going to Atlanta. The whites must stay firm in their conscience. We blacks must see that they do. If Martin Luther King's death doesn't unite us, all of us are committing to suicide.

ABOVE AND OPPOSITE Mourners

"SOME BAD-ASS MOTHERS who don't buy whitey's shit." This was the high praise for the Black Panthers from disciples in black ghettos across the nation. Aflame with racial unrest, the turbulent year 1969 was burning furiously as I entered the Panther headquarters on Shattuck Street in Berkeley, California. The back stairwell was dark, and the young man leading me had fallen quiet. But the Marxist theories he had bombarded me with en route from San Francisco still rang in my ears. As we climbed, the darkness grew fragrant with the odor of cooking. At the top of the stairs the young Panther gave the door three quick raps, waited, then gave four more. The door opened to a kitchen brimming with men, women, and children who had come to share a supper of rabbit stew. David Hilliard, the party's chief of staff, was at the stove, stirring the contents of a large pot. He observed me through dark glasses. "Welcome, brother. Be with you in a minute." He nodded toward two men standing in a

OPPOSITE Child and Doll, North Carolina, circa 1980
ABOVE Black Panther Headquarters, Berkeley, California, 1969

doorway. "Donald Cox, our field marshal, and my brother June." They nodded. I glanced about the room. In spite of all the people, it was strangely quiet. Tension was in the faces, even in those of the children. Something was wrong.

After the bowls were filled Hilliard ushered me into a back room where his brother and Cox joined us. Cox broke the silence. "What have you come here to do, brother?"

"To show your side of the story."

"That means hanging out with us, taking chances. Our lives are on the line. The pigs are trying to wipe us out."

"I know. That's why I'm here."

"Do you think that honky magazine you work for will print what we have to say?"

"That's just another chance we have to take."

He gave me a hard look, took a crumpled sheaf of paper from his pocket and handed it to me. "Read that, brother."

Newswoman Being Frisked at Black Panther Headquarters in Berkeley, California, 1968

> *Weapons to be employed:* Rifles, shotguns, 33-MM gas guns, 37-MM grenade launchers and Thompson machine guns. *The assault plans:* Assign two-man squad to front with shotgun (solid slugs) and armor-piercing rifle to blast armor plate off upper windows. Upper shields to be shot out, and use 00 buckshot to shoot out all lower windows. Use rifle slugs to try and knock open main front door. Front and back guard lay down fire on the second floor. Assault squad (three men) armed with machine guns approach building from the south. Squad enter building through front broken windows and doors. Two men enter and move left and to right center of ground floor. Fire thirty rounds each up through the second story floor, and reload. The entire building should then be flooded with tear gas. The entire upper floor should be covered with intense fire. Assault squad will then proceed upstairs and bring down the wounded and dead. *The target:* The Black Panther Party headquarters on Shattuck Street in Berkeley. *The task force:* (in the event of a disturbance at the Panther Party office). The Berkeley police.

My thoughts returned to the kitchen; to the women and children. "This is incredible."

"The pigs are incredible."

I put the memorandum on the wire to *Life*'s New York Bureau the next morning. It wired back: SORRY — WITHOUT PROOF THE DOCUMENT IS UNPRINTABLE."

I cabled again: CHECK OUT STATEMENT WITH CHIEF BAKER [Berkeley Police Chief], THEN WIRE BACK SOONEST.

The answer: NO OUTRIGHT DENIAL FROM BAKER. PROCEED WITH CAUTION. GOOD LUCK.

For the next three weeks I rode with the Panthers night and day — with police watching our every move. At night their headlights stayed glued to our rear window. A rainstorm was blowing one night. I sat in the backseat with the young Marxist who had brought me to the Panther headquarters. Glares from a squad car's headlamps stayed on us. Turning, he squinted into it. "The filthy pigs. Man, I'd like to blow those fuckers away."

"They would probably like doing the same thing to us."

"No doubt about that. I just finished your book *A Choice of Weapons*. Would you write it the same way today?"

"I would. Why do you ask?"

"With those pigs' guns trained on our ass? I can't believe you, man."

Cox was driving. Hilliard was beside him in the front seat. Somewhat annoyed, I said, "Friend, you've got a .45 automatic on your lap. I've got a 35-millimeter camera on mine — and I feel my weapon is more powerful than yours." His derisive smile urged me on. "My ass is hanging out here with yours. If they start firing, I go the way you go. So don't give me that bullshit." He didn't answer. I didn't know whether his silence was in my favor or not. I acted as though I didn't care, but I did.

I knew where my Harvard-trained antagonist was coming from. Karl Marx had been the party's Messiah since its inception. But to young blacks, who were being clubbed, slammed against walls, and frisked everyday, a lecture about dialectical materialism was like talk without words. Each nightfall I went back to my hotel relieved to have arrived without mishap. I fail to remember my antagonist's name. I do recall his being shot in a police ambush several weeks later — dying with a reckless show of courage inspired by the ideology of a German socialist.

By 1970 the Panthers were in deep trouble. Huey Newton, their leader, was in prison at San Luis Obispo, serving fifteen years for killing a policeman. Bobby Seale, another party leader, was in jail fighting extradition to Connecticut, where he would be charged for the murder of ex-Panther Alex Rackley. Twenty-one others were imprisoned in New York for alleged bombings. In Chicago fourteen policemen had shot up a Panther's apartment, killing Fred Hampton and Mark Clark. Now they were raiding other Panther homes.

Eldridge Cleaver, the party's embittered spokesman, had fled to Algiers with his wife, Kathleen, and their five-month-old son, Maceo. Two months later I flew to Algiers in search of Cleaver. I found him in a yellowish five-room house on the Mediterranean coast. Visiting with him and his family were three other party members — Emory Davis, the Panthers' minister of culture, his wife, Judy, and Connie Matthews, who represented the party in Scandinavia. In a small hall was the "workshop," with two typewriters, a mimeograph machine, and stacks of printing paper. There was very little laughter in that house. Most was talk about revolution and death. It was the cluttered shelter of a man on the run. Bags stayed packed.

For several days Cleaver roared defiance against Babylon, his name for America. During our final meeting I showed him press clippings about the police killings of Fred Hampton and Mark Clark. "Well, what do you think?" I asked.

"Pure unadulterated crap. We have to be shot up in our homes before the press becomes indignant. We have charged the pigs with murder over and over again. Now, after twenty-eight murders, the press finally takes a look. Those murders have to be avenged. The pigs have to be punished in the same way they committed the crimes."

Quietly Kathleen agreed. "Right on, Papa Rage."

"Did you know that Roy Wilkins and Arthur Goldberg are forming an investigating committee of their own?"

"It's too late for their concern. Those brothers are dead. Concern won't stop bullets. The problem's still there. It's our right to defend our homes. When the pigs bust through the door, put a gun in their faces and say, 'Split, mothers.'"

"Black moderates — what do you offer them?"

"Nothing. Not even condolences. They'll bring their own death through apathy." His anger was building. Getting up from his chair, he walked to a window and stared into the darkness. He was a big man, well over six feet, broad-shouldered and powerfully built. "Violence! Our people are programmed into violence by Uncle Sam! Black boys should be shooting the Reagans, Wallaces, and Nixons instead of Korean and Vietnamese boys!" After a few moments of silence he said softly, "I was right next to little Bobby Hutton when the pigs murdered him. It's amazing that they didn't rub me out too. Instead they slammed me into Vacaville with a shot-up leg and revoked my parole without a hearing. Then, after freeing me on a habeas corpus, they trumped up more charges to send me back to prison. Had I gone back they would have killed me. So I split."

"Are you ever coming back?"

"I'm just on vacation from Babylon. Two-seven-seven Pine's still my address." He turned, looked me hard in the eye. "Would you consider serving the Black Panther Party as their minister of information?" His offer left me ruffled, searching for an answer.

"I'm truly honored, Eldridge, but —"

"We need you more than the establishment does."

"Certainly you realize that, as a journalist, I would lose all credibility."

"Give it some thought. Just remember that we are disciplined revolutionaries who hate violence."

Looking back, I find myself displeased with my reply. Both of us were caught up in the truth of the black man's ordeal. I recognized his scars and acknowledged my own. Yet, we had met over a deep chasm of time, the events of which forged different weapons for us. If

I had been twenty at the time, I might have joined the Panthers. Then maybe not. As a boy I was taught to take the first lick before fighting back. Things were different now. A fist wasn't a bullet. I too would have shot a cop, or anyone else, who forced his way into my house to kill me or one of my family.

I still prefer changing things without violence — provided violence is not thrust upon me. If this was truly the position of the Black Panthers, then their weapons and mine were not irreconcilable.

It was a wet, windswept night when I left Cleaver. His last words to me were about social justice: "the kind that turns a blind eye to a man's color." Martin Luther King had been murdered while seeking the same thing. Martyrdom, in Cleaver's case, would be easy to come by. I left wondering if I would ever see him alive again.

He came back. But today Bobby Seale, his cohort during those days, refuses to speak to him; refers to him as a traitor to the principles of the Black Panther Party. Kathleen, his once loyal wife, deserted him to get a law degree at Harvard. Before Huey Newton was stabbed to death in 1989, I talked to him by telephone. "Where can I find Cleaver?" I asked.

"I avoid Mr. Milquetoast. You'll probably find him breaking bread at some racist Mormon Church. Joining that bigoted outfit was like joining the Ku Klux Klan." Time and circumstance had wiped out Cleaver's rageful past.

Muhammad Ali

MUHAMMAD ALI'S FLINTY TONGUE had put him on a multitude of burial lists when I visited him in the summer of 1970. He was at a gym in Miami training for his upcoming fight with Henry Cooper in London. "Dance, baby, dance," Angelo Dundee, his trainer, purred from the ringside. Floating, ducking, pounding his sparring partner with a staccato of fast combinations, Ali was working hard. Then, to show that he was fit, he allowed his sparring mate to bull him about as Cooper might do. Later, on the rubdown table, he searched for praise from Angelo. "Could I have whupped Joe Louis and Jack Johnson in their time?"

"Baby, you could have whipped everybody in anybody's time."

That's the way things went every day. At his house later that afternoon, he downed a huge steak, stretched out on a couch, and began reading a newspaper. He had resisted the draft. And to that newspaper he was no longer just a loudmouth kid but "a shameless traitor, a bigot and a bum." Surly and tired, he flung the paper into a corner. "I ain't got no quarrel with the Vietcong. Those white devils can burn in hell! Ain't hurting the gates none, just making it harder on their white hopes!" He turned to me. "Why'd you come down here to old hot Miami?"

"Trying to find out if you're as obnoxious as they say you are."

He laughed. "I'm worse, brother. I'm a bad, terrible, awful, cruel black man who won't do what the white man wants him to do. That's why they call me all those names." He reached up and turned on the radio. Sam Cooke had wailed out his latest hit, "Shake," when the announcer's voice cut in: "Cassius Clay is back in town training for his —" Ali twisted the dial, shutting him off in mid-sentence. "Cassius Clay! Cassius Clay! I'm on everybody's lips but they won't call me by my right name." He slammed a fist into the palm of his right hand. "Pressure and strain. When you're controversial like me, everybody and his brother tries to burn you!"

"Why set yourself up for it? You've got what you want now. Why not cool it?"

After several moments of silence he said, "People don't ask me to speak at places like they used to. Martin Luther King was the only black leader who sent me a telegram when I became champion of the world."

"You're young yet. They'll come around."

"I aim to go on doing just like I've been doing. I don't owe nobody nothing but Elijah Muhammad. I owe him my life."

I was leaving the next day. It was now or never, so I stuck my neck out. "It's not only the whites. A lot of black people don't like the way you act, or the way you go around preaching hate."

This cut him deeper than I expected. "I've got more important things to do than hatin' white folks. I'm teaching black kids about Elijah Muhammad, and getting myself ready to destroy Cooper. Don't hate lions and tigers either, but I know they bite. The white man's got everything going for him — White Swan Soap, White Owl Cigars, Snow White and

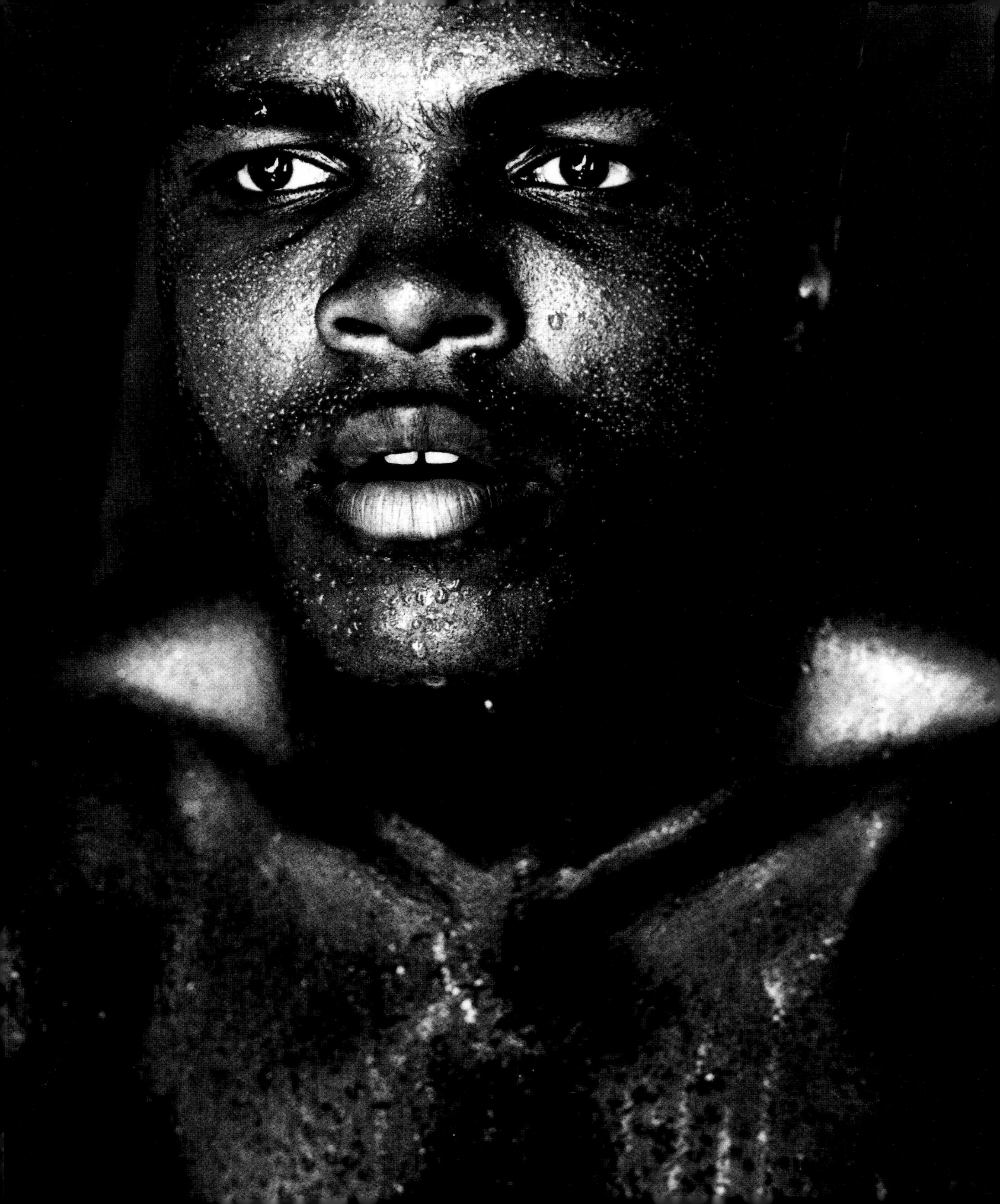

her little white dwarfs — why's he worryin' about me?"

"What about your draft situation?"

"Elijah Muhammad tells us to pray five times a day. What time does that give me to kill somebody? A couple of years back the army said I was a nut of some kind. Now they've decided I'm smart without even testin' me again. I don't even know where Vietnam is — and I ain't going lookin' for it. I ain't killin' nobody unless they come over here and try to kill me. I'm tellin' you like it is."

Ali had made his point. He was now the world's heavyweight champion. Did that give him the responsibility to think or act differently? A lot of people thought it did. I wasn't too sure. I would have backed up my son David had he resisted going to Vietnam. I left Ali that evening, not expecting to see him again. But early the next morning he came to drive me to the airport. At the gate he said, "I don't want to do anything to hurt my people. I've been doing a lot of thinking since our talk yesterday. I hope you're gonna be in London with me."

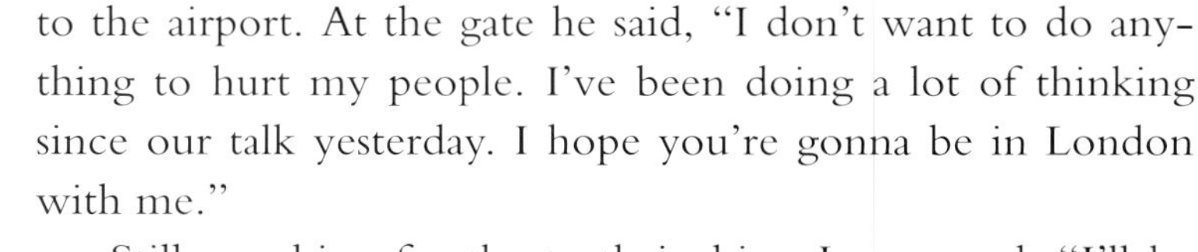

Still searching for the truth in him, I answered, "I'll be there." And I left hoping that one day I would be as proud of him as I was of Joe Louis. In London I witnessed the destruction of Cooper. Afterward at a press conference, Ali said, "Now that I have done what I came here to do, I'm going back home." *Home*. He said it in a way that rang softly of contrition. A new and great black hero was slowly emerging.

Time and brutal combat have reduced his voice to a mumble that is close to silence. But the thorns have been digested and the heart, once seething, is no longer angry. He remains sociable but now his eyes do most of the talking. Undoubtedly the bad times still hang in his memory, and one gets the feeling that a question mark hovers above everything spoken to him. His eyes answer, "I know, I know," and their twinkling is often accompanied by an obscure smile. I often think back to his days of travail; to his hours of triumph. Lumped together they bring back some memorable advice I read somewhere or another: "Don't bury a man before death catches up with him."

Portrait Gallery

WITH CHASTE EYES, some sitters and some cameras can say yes or no without realizing what the other has on its mind. The sitter, somewhat skeptical, looks into the camera, asking, "Do you know who I really am?" The camera, in search of an answer, stares at the face, the mannerisms, the clothes — even the shoes and socks, then does whatever it feels like doing. Since both sitter and camera are capable of deception, the truth can disappear within seconds. Lately, I have come to view portraits as images that invariably leave a lot of questions unanswered. Yet there are some memorable ones taken by certain photographers that assume an inexhaustible presence — staying on and on to find their rightful place in pictorial history. But early enough I discovered something about sitters who appear to be bathed in self-idolatry. Completely unaware of being at the camera's mercy, they often turn it into a sharp-edged sword that can murder them away with glee.

The moments I spent making these portraits always flow back with the warmest of memories. They are of people I have admired and felt at ease with. And, in most cases, I attempted to intertwine their personalities with their professions. The responsibility of breaking down any barriers that stood between them and my camera belonged to me. Since each of them seemed comfortable with my presence, I didn't experience any problems. I remain grateful for having shared time with them.

Adam Clayton Powell, New York, 1948

ABOVE Langston Hughes, Chicago, 1941
OPPOSITE Marva Louis, Chicago, 1941

Leon Kirchner, New York, 1955

Alexander Liberman, 1948

Joseph Welch, Boston, 1954

Samuel Barber, New York, 1955

Aaron Copland, New York, 1955

Alberto Giacometti, Paris, 1951

OPPOSITE Leo Lerman, New York, 1948
ABOVE Leonard Bernstein, New York, 1955

Alan Hovhaness, New York, 1955

Alexander Calder, 1952

ABOVE Jo Davidson, New York, 1948
OPPOSITE Gloria Vanderbilt, New York, 1960

Color Gallery II

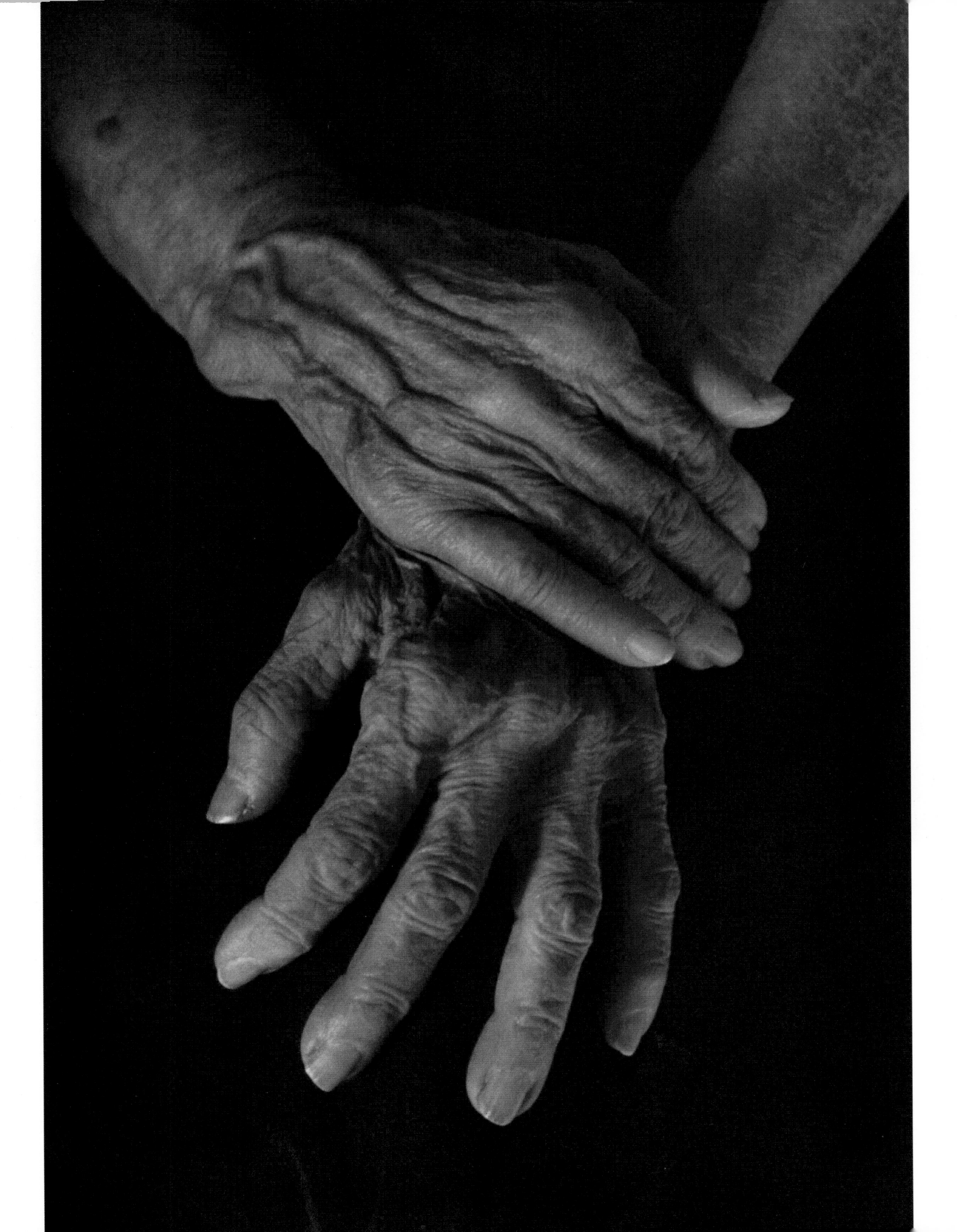

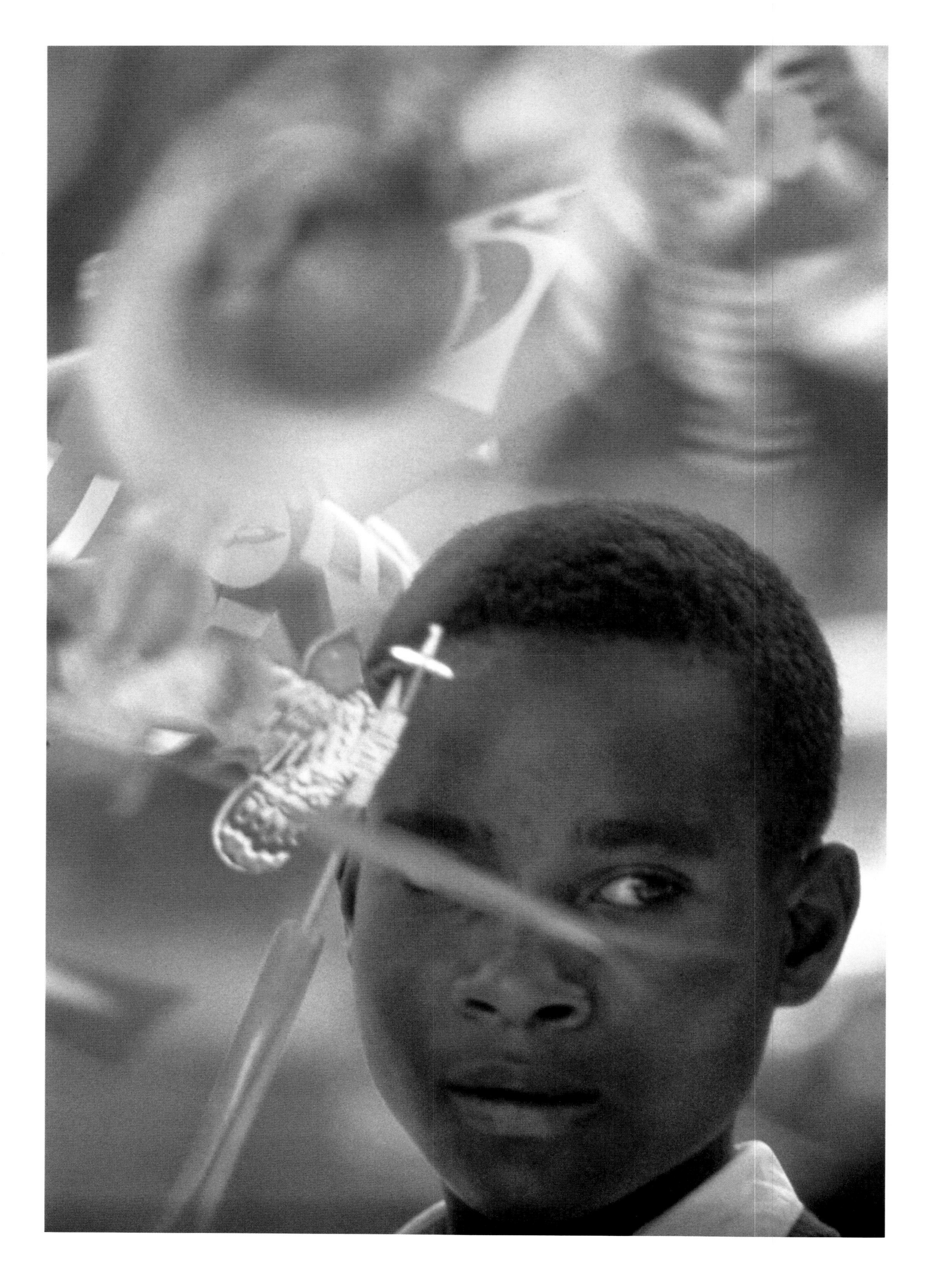

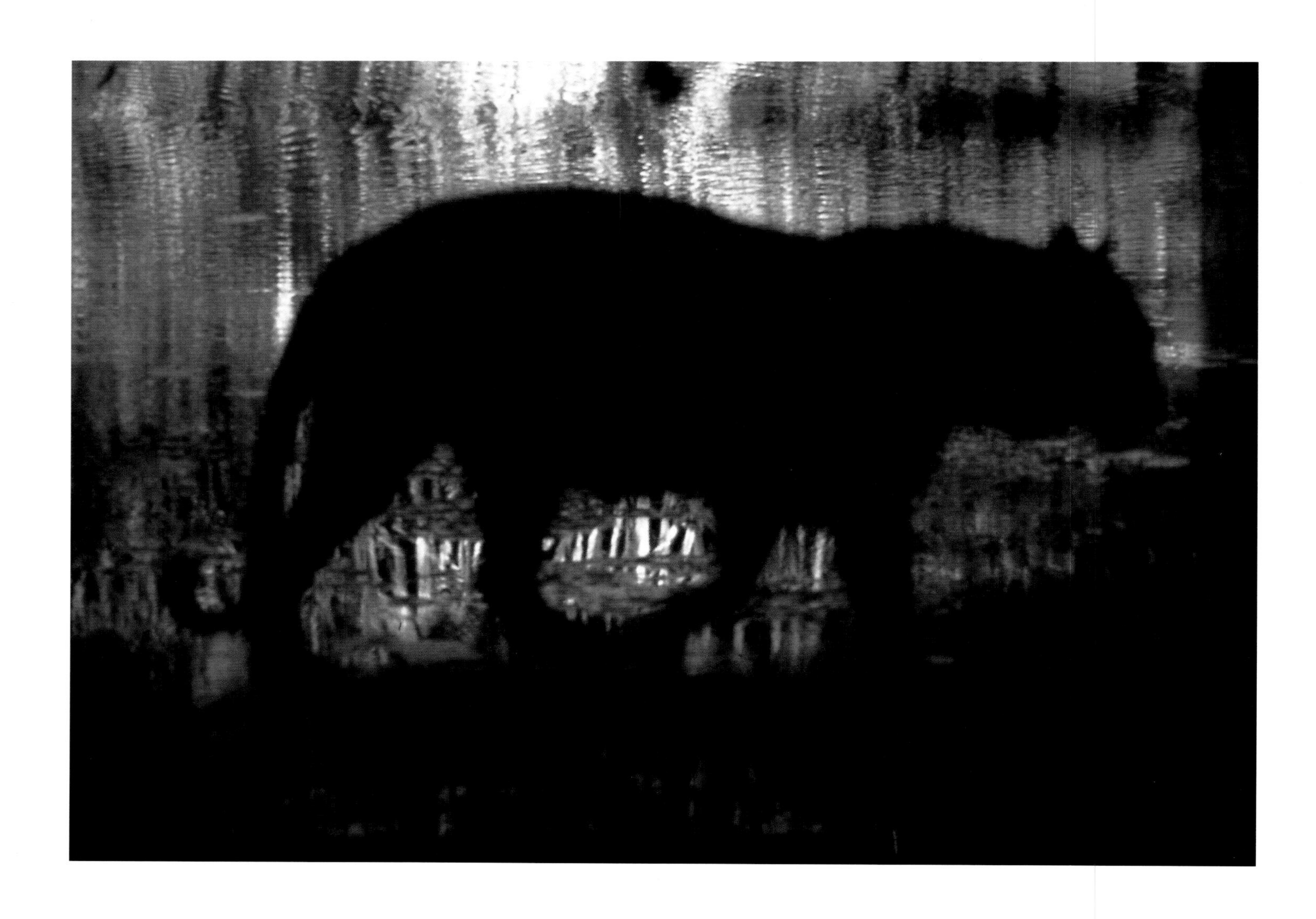

THE Patio

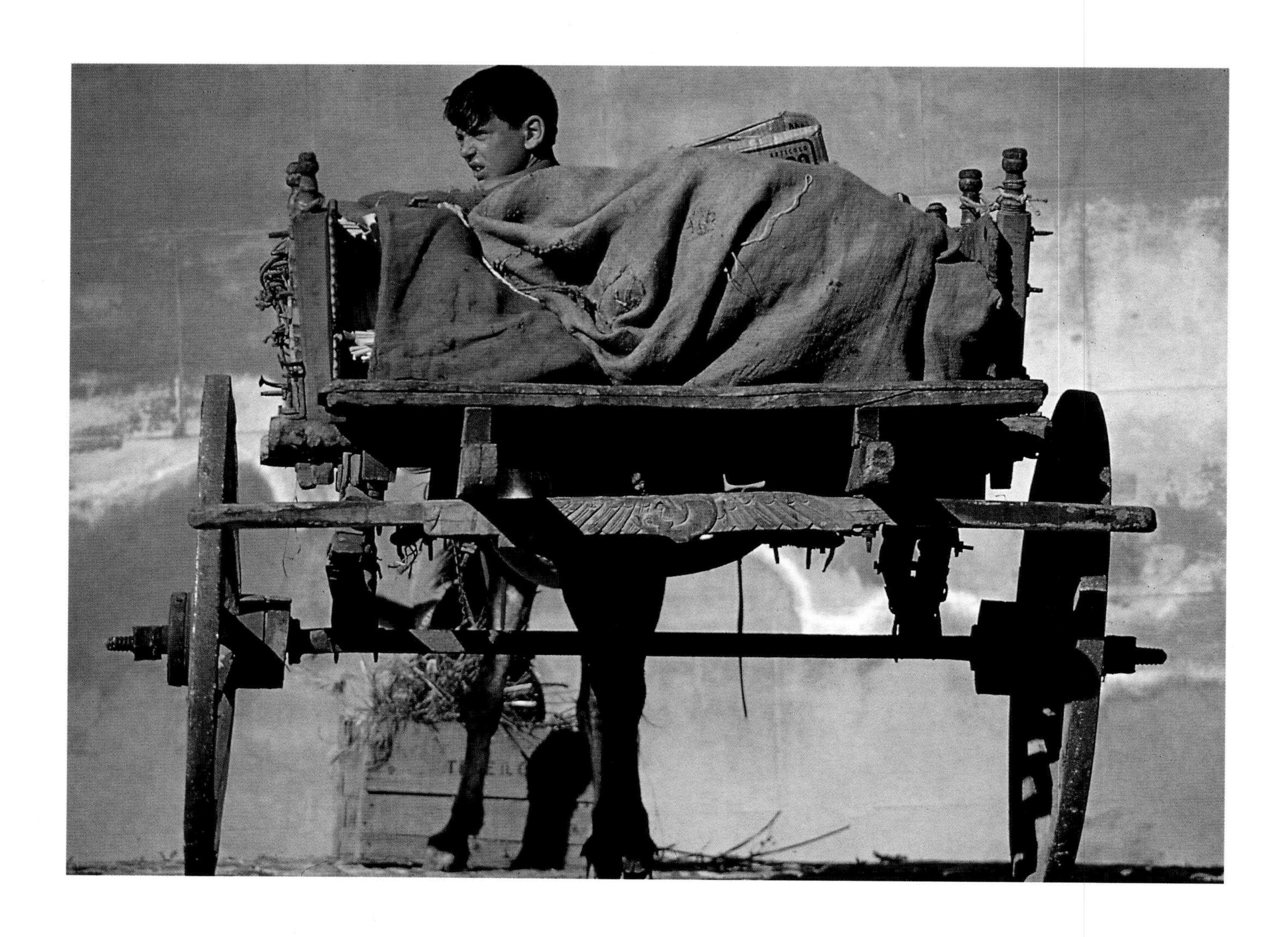

Motion Pictures — and the Family

I HAD KNOCKED. Hollywood's closed doors to black directors had opened with *The Learning Tree.* Now *Shaft,* a noisy film about a black, suave, high-powered big-city detective, was offered to me by MGM — a grand leap from the Kansas prairies to the mean streets of New York. The screenplay told me that I would be swapping sombreros, and in a questionable way. Should I forget that door that took so long to open, or the possibility of its abruptly closing? There was no set precedent to give me counsel. Finally, after deciding that perhaps it was something I shouldn't do, I signed a contract and did it.

Soon after *Shaft* was completed, Jim Aubrey, MGM's top executive, hustled me off to London for a showing to the British press. The variety of questions that followed the showing kept my conscience smiling.

"I say, what's the meaning of the word *shaft?"*

"Well — well, you might say it means *up yours."*

"And one bloke calling another *mother.* What gives there?"

With several ladies in the audience, I was left with the only answer that would spare them humiliation. "All — well, six other letters were left out — but I feel they are better left unsaid. However, I admit that they begin with the letter *f."*

Shaft premiered on New York's Broadway in 1971. I was home asleep when the phone rang at one in the morning. It was my son David.

"Dad! Get up and come over here!"

"David, are you out of your mind? It's one o'clock!"

"Get over here, Dad. You won't believe what I'm seeing!"

I gave in, dressed, and, after reaching the theater, I saw what justified his excitement. Two city blocks were filled with people waiting in line for tickets. Soon it was like this throughout the country. Within the next three months, John Shaft spread his presence throughout the universe. Now, with the door flung open, other black directors could look forward to being ensconced in Hollywood's lucrative parlors.

Then came *Shaft's Big Score!* (1972), *The Super Cops* (1974), *Leadbelly* (1976), and *Solomon Northup's Odyssey* (1984). With *Leadbelly,* I began living among thorns. Frank Yablins, the studio's head, was suddenly fired just after it was completed, and Barry Diller, who took over, became the most excruciating thorn. Devoting himself to *Lipstick* — a bomb — he lent no support to *Leadbelly,* although the *Los Angeles Times* critic Charles Champlan hailed it as one of the best films of the year. Nearly two years of effort had been put into the filming, the editing, and the musical score. A telephone call from a friend in San Francisco pushed me to the brink. "Your film," he said, "opened here at a local porno house." Frustrated, I packed up and fled that insane place.

During those last twelve months Genevieve and I had seen very little of each other. By now she had become a vice president at J. B. Lippincott, and her work there had doubled. She handled it well and I was proud of her. But some destructive force was constantly snipping at our relationship. Hostility fired our conversation to a boiling point one night, and the moment turned on us. She went to our bed alone; I slept in the living room. She dressed for work in silence the next morning; and in that silence we both knew that it was over. From that morning on, we didn't have much to say to one another. At the end of the month, she left. I loved her still. In my den her wedding bouquet, the last vestige of our vows, was also crumbling. Reluctantly, I placed it in a wastepaper basket.

There was no sweeter time than that of acknowledging my eldest son's success as motion-picture director. Gordon Jr.'s films, *Super Fly, Aaron Loves Angela,* and *Three the Hard Way,* were feeding his aspirations. He was in Kenya, making his fourth film. At half-past three one morning in 1979, the telephone snapped me awake. Nairobi was calling. The voice of Jimmy Richardson, Gordon's assistant, came over the line. "Pops — something terrible just happened."

As though I knew, I spoke the most painful words I've ever spoken. "Gordon's dead."

"You're right, Pops. I'm sorry."

"What happened, Jimmy?" I wanted to know — while dreading to know.

"His plane spun in during takeoff. Three others went down with him."

I said all that was left to say. "I'll get there right away."

"Don't come. There was an intense fire. Nothing's left but ashes."

Ashes. My son — shapeless smoldering ashes. The terrible imagery wavered through my thoughts, refusing to leave. "Jimmy — take some to spread on Kilimanjaro. He loved that mountain. And be sure to bring some home."

I dressed with a deliberate slowness. No need to hurry such news to his wife, whose stomach bulged with an unborn child. She gasped after opening the door. My early unexpected arrival, with a face showing such despair, had struck her instantly. "Oh, Good Lord," she moaned. "Something's happened to Gordon. I know it!"

"Yes, Leslie, he died in a plane crash."

Distraught, with her hands clasping her stomach, she collapsed into my arms. "This poor child inside me will never know its father." She was still weeping when I left three hours later. Back at home I reluctantly went to the telephone and made calls to Sally, Gordon's mother, his sister and brother, Toni and David. Toni's son, Alain, was away at school. Now each of them would also have to suffer the pain of this terrible morning.

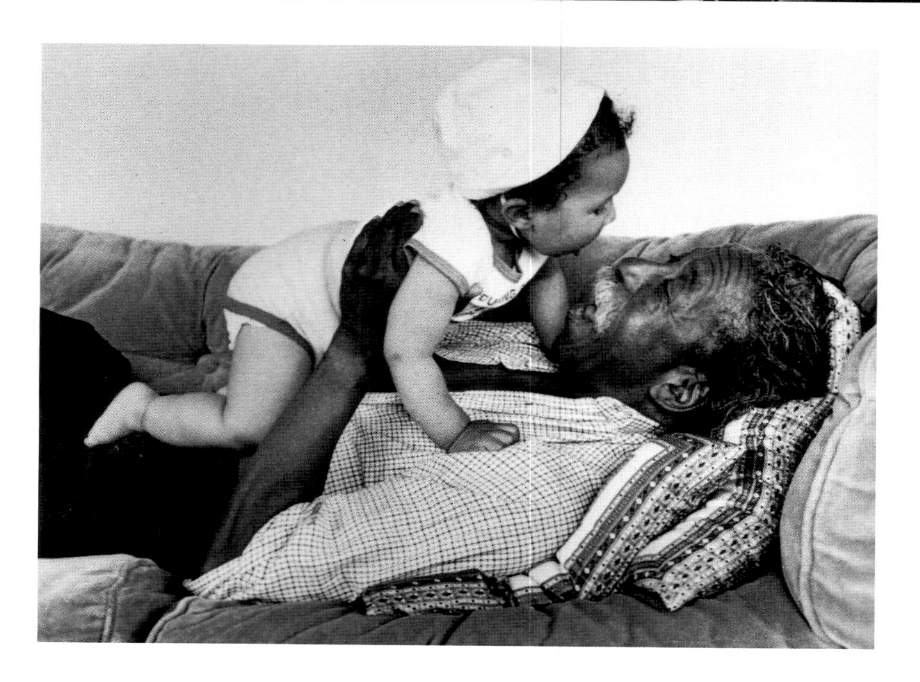

TOP LEFT Leslie, Gordon Jr.'s wife, and Gordon III
TOP RIGHT Gordon Jr., Cannes, France
BOTTOM LEFT Author listens as son Gordon Jr. plays guitar
Photograph by Robert Lucas
BOTTOM RIGHT Author and grandson Gordon III
Photograph by Jill Krementz

Three years passed. Gordon III, Gordon Jr.'s son, landed on my chest and awakened me from sleep. Lifting my moustache he said, "Pepe, I've never seen your lips before." Then, in a somewhat puzzling way he added, "but I've never seen my father either."

He is seventeen now. His father's ashes still rest in a small bottle on a shelf in my den. For years I had awaited that moment when I would find the courage to show them to him. When at last I did he stared at them, saying softly, "So that's my father. He's been here with us all the time." Then, for several strained moments, we sat in silence beneath the picture of his father looking down from a bookshelf. During those moments the spirit of Gordon Jr. seemed to hover above us — flowing with verse from my favorite poet, Pablo Neruda.

When they wish to see me, now they know —
they must look for me where I am not,
and if they have voice and time left over,
they can have a talk with my portrait.

Suddenly my grandson asked, "What was your father like?"

"Strong, kind, soft-spoken, and religious. Poppa was a fine man."

I then recounted one of his unforgettable acts. Without consulting my mother, he had gone to the hospital and had skin stripped from his back and thighs to aid a small girl who was seriously burned in a fire. "Jackson, why would you do such a thing without telling me first?" Momma had asked.

"No matter, Sarah. You'd have said yes in any case." Years later I asked him if the child's parents had sent flowers or thanked him. His reply left me slightly embarrassed. "Not as I recall. But I didn't do it for flowers or thanks. I did it for the child."

Over supper I found myself saying once more, "Yep, Poppa was a fine man." I was wishing that my grandson could have known him — and certainly his own father as well.

Most unexpectedly, the letter from Sara floated in from a small town up in Maine. Enclosed were photographs of her and her three-year-old daughter, Dannah. Both were beautiful. The letter was explicit. Sara, twenty-four at the time she wrote me, had been adopted at birth, but for years she had secretly, but relentlessly, searched for her real parents. At last she had found her biological mother, who had, just a few days before, pointed to a photograph of me in a magazine and said calmly, "Sara, that is your grandfather."

The letter was tender, mildly desperate, and ended with a plea: "I'm told that your son David is my father. I would deeply appreciate your showing him this letter."

I read and reread the letter, looked at the photographs over and over again. My son's features, deeply etched into her's, spoke the truth. David was a father. I was a great-grandfather. I sent the letter and pictures on to David in Texas. Without waiting for his answer, I telephoned her. "Sara, this is your grandfather Gordon."

Several moments of silence passed before she answered. "I knew you would call. I'm happy, so happy."

"I'm happy too, Sara. We must see one another as soon as possible. I sent your letter on to David in Texas."

"Do you think he will call?"

"I'm sure he will. Give him time. All this will be new to him, you know." There wasn't much more to say between a granddaughter and grandfather who had never realized each other existed. David called Sara, then me. "She sounds wonderful, Dad."

She came for a weekend to visit, then to the premiere of my ballet, *Martin,* in Washington, D.C. There she eased gracefully into the heart of our family. Later, she asked to accompany me on a trip I was taking to London. Since both of us longed to make up for the years lost between us, I took her. On the plane I looked at Sara. She was asleep with contentment on her face. Photographs of Dannah and her newly born son, Hans Christian, lay in my hands. I was no longer a missing grandparent.

To me, my children and grandchildren are like a gathering of fine jewels. *"Pepe,"* they call me, and the sound of the word always rings with love. Alain seems to be emerging as the keeper of the flame. Devoted to preserving the fruits of my efforts, he stays close, attending to those gnawing problems that spin around me nowadays. Since he has taken on this obligation, I have more time for looking toward the future. He, Gordon III, and I shared an unusual experience recently. The two of them sat talking. At the piano, with a pipe in my mouth, I struggled with a passage that had, along with the pipe smoke, troubled me for months. The passage was at last surrendering to my fingers when I inhaled two whiffs of that smoke. Then, suffering another vertiginous attack, I went to lie down. That pipe, a friend for so many years, had become my enemy. I got up and joined my grandsons. And, somewhat astonished, they watched as I broke that old friend's neck over my knee.

TOP LEFT Sara Lagerstrom, author's granddaughter
Photograph by John Ferris
TOP RIGHT Author's son, David Parks, tank gunner in Vietnam
Photograph by U.S. Army
BOTTOM LEFT Author with great-granddaughter, Dannah Lagerstrom
Photograph by Toni Parks
BOTTOM RIGHT Hans Christian Lagerstrom, author's great-grandson
Photograph by Carol Dana

ARMENIAN, CHEROKEE, CHINESE, ENGLISH, French, Iraeli, Scottish, Swedish, and Yugoslavian. This is the jumble of bloodlines that, through wedlock or other ways, flowed into my family and left it the color of a rainbow. Happiness hasn't prevailed in every case, but the differences of skin color had nothing to do with that. Absolute serenity in most households is an illusion of our daily existence. As kin to those of foreign birth, I've tried living up to what they wished me to be. And I assume they have attempted to acknowledge what I expected of them. To my own list of worthy acquisitions add three mothers-in-law, one of African descent, one from Sweden, and yet another one, from Shanghai. While serving as a consul general for Chiang Kai-shek, my Chinese father-in-law, C. K. Young, was assassinated by the Japanese long before I married his daughter, Gene. Had he lived I hope he would not have found cause for misreading me.

So, a glance back at my past tells me that I, like my children, have experienced kinships with a good number of nationalities. And I have no interest in the opinions of anyone who would differ with our choices. Finally, through years of assimilation, this, my family, emerges as one huge kaleidoscope. Aglow with the hues of so many different skins, it can rightfully claim that title.

TOP Sally Alvis Parks, author's first wife
MIDDLE RIGHT Author's eldest daughter, Toni Parks, then Toni Brouillaud
Photograph by Jean-Luc Brouillaud
MIDDLE LEFT Author with grandson Alain Brouillaud, Toni's son
Photograph by Esther Bubley
BOTTOM RIGHT Derek Parsons, Toni's husband
Photograph by Toni Parks
BOTTOM LEFT Author's grandsons, Alain Brouillaud and Gordon III

TOP LEFT Elizabeth Campbell Parks, author's second wife
TOP RIGHT Leslie Parks, author's youngest daughter, at graduation from Hackley School
BOTTOM LEFT Vivian Campbell, Elizabeth Campbell Parks's mother
BOTTOM RIGHT Author and daughter Leslie Parks

TOP LEFT Mr. and Mrs. C. K. Young, Gene Young Parks's father and mother
TOP RIGHT Author's wife Gene Young Parks, at premiere of his film *Shaft*
Photograph by MGM
BOTTOM Author and his third wife, Gene Young Parks
Photograph by Jill Krementz

Recent Work

RECENTLY, AS IF FLEEING FROM THE PAST, my camera has been caught up in images lending themselves to horizons of my imagination. And, for me, this venture has become a matter of devout observance, a sort of metamorphosis that extends my vision to plateaus I didn't know existed. But at times, after a little talk with myself, I'm left with an uneasy question: "Is your impatience with nature urging you to create natural forces to your own liking?" Good question, I admit. But the next day comes on with my resolve burning like dry wood, diminishing the importance of the enigma. I go on — in pursuit of my own hills, mountains, and valleys; of prehistoric birds winging the heights over unlikely places; of landscapes grown pale under swirling fog. Clouds, unraveled by the wind, become white patches afloat in the sky. Crumpling leaves became wreaths of finery. The sun bursts through with its atomic mane. Flower petals fly like birds through the sky. The moon becomes a saucer from which I eat, and a fallen leaf is food for my table. Like souls touching, poetry, music, paint, and the camera keep calling, and I can't bring myself to say no. All these things have become like alien wonders, beckoning. And finding no need to ask pardon of myself, I pursue them. Their mystery is as inescapable as air is from the wind.

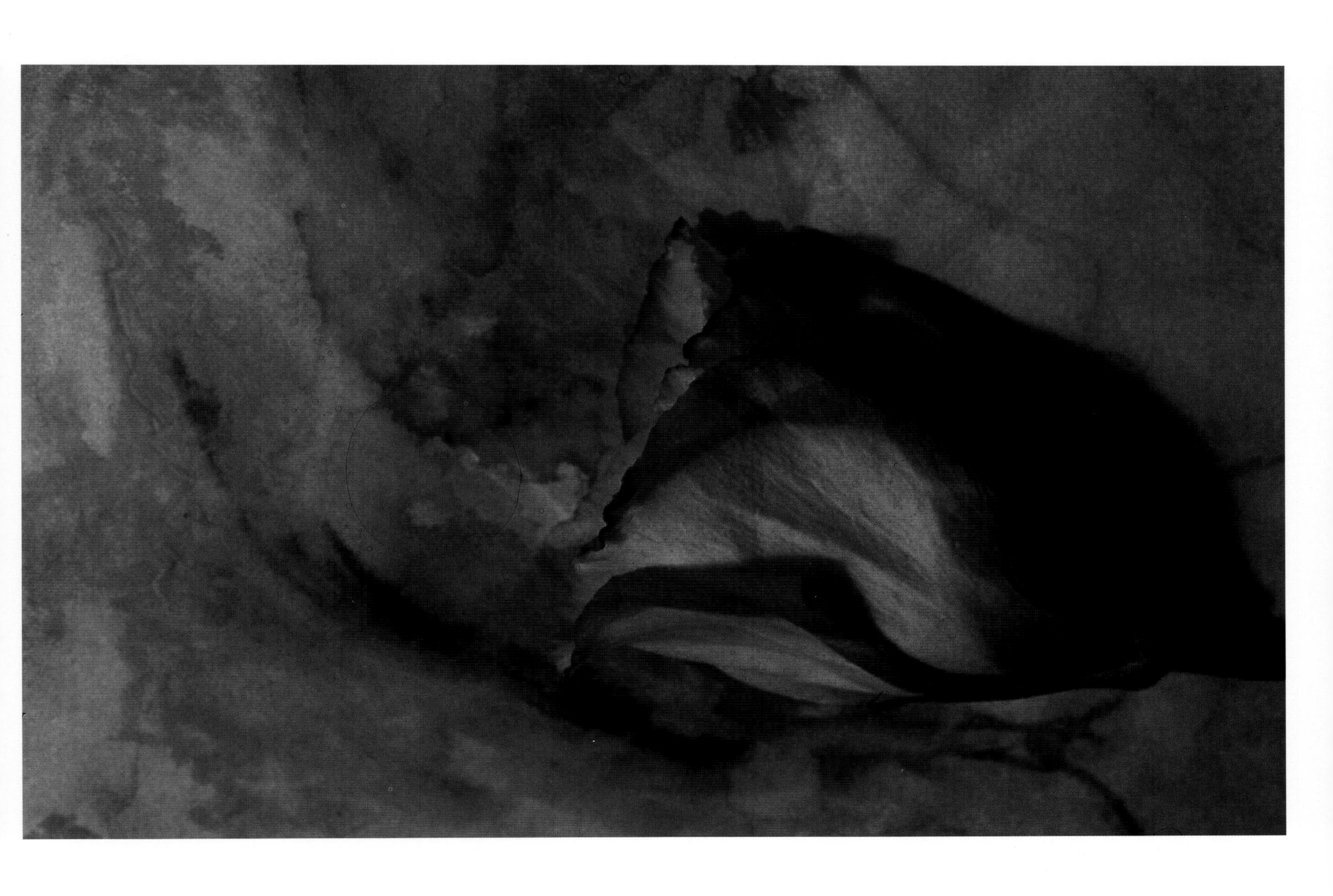

Epilogue

WITH ALL THE YEARS PASSED, my life seems like a long disjointed dream. Time still spreads its wings over me, but certainly I acknowledge the windfalls of aging. Yet I'm finding signs of time left over — unused time, beckoning me away from the finish line. With everything I've worked for coming together at last, I still feel somewhat at sea. Dreams keep moving in, and the desire is still there to devour them. Compelling me is the need to compensate providence for granting space to me upon this planet. And, since my time is so short, there is no room for idleness. At the moment I'm painting, reworking an unfinished novel, editing verse, and composing a piano sonata that reflects the natures of my four children. Naturally, the camera moves in to have its say now and then.

"Any major regrets?" I'm often asked. Yes, a huge one that troubles me constantly. I deeply lament Momma and Poppa's absence. Since their love and sacrifice gave shape to my dreams and hopes, they deserved to know that I've tried not to fail them. Dying with a smile, my sister Gladys promised to tell them about all my striving. If that promise was kept, I have no regrets to add. I believed in Gladys. She, like all my other brothers and sisters, "died with a soul ready to die well." I, the last, am hoping to do the same.

Meanwhile, time moves on, eating my days as though they were ripened plums. Eventually I too will drop, exhausted. But, for the moment, the contentment that most mornings offer gives me good reason to smile at what tomorrow might bring. I recall the marriages to Sally, Elizabeth, and Genevieve as magnificent years — though our divorces were like partings within shrouded shadows. But our finest days together seem to have set a rule — decreeing that none of us should have to walk alone. And that's the way things are. I will be beside them if they need me. And, if I should need them, I know they will be there for me. Somehow each of us has allowed that discerning rule to overlook our differences. Where once discord existed, a tangible togetherness stays on to replace it.

Often I think back to Miss McClintok, a white high school teacher in Kansas. As an adviser to black students, she gave us some disheartening advice: "Don't waste your parents' money on college. You'll wind up as porters and maids. To graduate from here is enough." To me, her advice went wanting. I didn't graduate, but when I was handed my thirtieth doctorate, I dedicated it to her — for pushing me to find her wrong. And without malice I regret that she wasn't present when, in 1986, I was chosen as Kansan of the Year. For that honor I am deeply grateful. Yet, between yesterday and today, I still wait impatiently for that segregated graveyard to become a forgotten memory. Until then, the peace, hovering between me and my birthplace, will continue to be untrustworthy.

At half past autumn I'm all roses, thorns, shadows, and dreams; still touching what exists; still weaving summer into those walls of winter. By now even the dust I walk through must have grown tired of my feet. But I keep moving; later is too late. I still have a passion for living and an undiminished ardor for womanhood. Recently, after running two miles, I bought a new tennis racquet and a faster pair of skis. They will tell me what I am — perhaps. Only the moon really knows me.

Unlocked Doors: Gordon Parks at the Crossroads BY PHILIP BROOKMAN

> Stories are for joining the past to the future. Stories are for those late hours in the night when you can't remember how you got from where you were to where you are. Stories are for eternity, when memory is erased, when there is nothing to remember except the story.[1] — *Tim O'Brien*

> How dare I consider my feelings superior to the gross environment that sought to claim me?[2] — *Richard Wright*

A PHOTOGRAPHER CAN BE STORYTELLER. Images of experience captured on film, when put together like words, can weave tales of feeling and emotion as bold as literature. Photographers have, after all, recorded the histories of the modern world: of people, landscapes, and even abstract concepts that only a camera might see. They bring together fact and fiction, experience, imagination, and feelings in a visual dialogue that has enormous impact on how we observe and relate to the external world and our internal selves.

Gordon Parks, then a young railroad worker riding the rails on the North Coast Limited between Chicago and Seattle, began to seriously consider the meaning of photography in 1937 at the age of twenty-five. At that time he was introduced to pictures made by a group of social documentary photographers for Franklin Delano Roosevelt's Farm Security Administration (FSA) Historical Section. The FSA was a seminal public-information project based in Washington, D.C. It was designed to call attention to the plight of the needy during the Depression and to create a historical record of social and cultural conditions across the country. The photographs that were created by the FSA between 1935 and 1942 influenced public opinion of the administration's New Deal policies. The picture file grew to more than sixty thousand images during these years, and the photographs were widely distributed; they were published in books, magazines, and newspapers throughout the country.

Parks first came across these FSA photographs in a magazine, and this discovery unlocked new doors for him to walk through.[3] He remembers vividly the names of photographers John Collier, Jack Delano, Walker Evans, Dorothea Lange, Russell Lee, Carl Mydans, Arthur Rothstein, Ben Shahn, and John Vachon, as well as the faces of dust bowl refugees in the pictures, "caught in their confusion and poverty." Parks also credits his experience of a dramatic newsreel film depicting an attack on a gunboat as one that solidified his interest in the medium. Such newslike images of current events brought history to life with "grim directness," animating the connections between suffering presented in the media, his feelings for other people, and his childhood memories of poverty.[4] "I was convinced of the power of a good picture," he thought at the time, seeking some means to turn his experiences into actions.[5] By absorbing the work of photographers and filmmakers in the late 1930s and early 1940s, he realized that visual communication could work as a language in ways that other expressive opportunities might not. Photography and film were for him personal and universal activities that postulated a mirror of experience; this discovery gave Parks a new way to tell stories about his own life, one with the potential to help make things better for others. He immediately spent $7.50 on a camera, then fell into the Puget Sound off Seattle while making his first amateur photographs of seagulls.

Like all African Americans of his generation, Parks grew up under the cloud of overt racism. Born in Fort Scott, Kansas, in 1912, he learned firsthand that success depended on real communication and the uncompromising development of his skills. His childhood memories and a curiosity about the world, coupled with the strong moral guidance of his parents, set the stage for a life of concern for others. "My mother had freed me from the curse of inferiority long before she died," Parks recalls, "by not allowing me to take refuge in the excuse that I was born black."[6] However, his personal struggles with indigence and bigotry as a youth later transformed his work as an artist. "I was born to a black childhood of confusion and poverty," he wrote, using the same words he found to describe the destitute farmers and their families in FSA pictures. "The memory of that beginning influences my work today."[7] It is this unique tension between his open embrace of these social issues and his transcendence of them that Parks harnessed to endow his work with didactic power. He would discover this process while photographing the people and streets of Washington, D.C., for the FSA.

Negro woman in her bedroom, Washington (southwest section), D.C., November 1942

Parks came of age in St. Paul, Minnesota, where he launched his photographic career making fashion pictures. By 1941 he began to learn more about documentary technique and produced a hard-hitting series focusing on social problems in Chicago. "The Saturday morning I started poking around the south side with my camera, I knew that more than anything else I wanted to strike at the evil of poverty," he remembers. "And here it was, under my feet, all around and above me. I could point the camera in any direction and record it. My own brush with it was motive enough."[8] He then accompanied Jack Delano on several FSA assignments in Chicago. In 1941 Russell Lee and Edwin Rosskam were also photographing the south side for *12 Million Black Voices,* Richard Wright's 1942 publication that was illustrated with numerous FSA images. Wright had gained national attention for *Native Son* in 1940.

Parks already sensed that he had to transcend his own feelings to reveal the spirit of the people and social problems he depicted. This important lesson took time to master. He discussed the issue of African American representation in art with the accomplished painter Charles White, who, like Parks, maintained a studio at the Southside Community Center. Responding directly to Parks's coverage of poverty in Chicago, Delano suggested that if support could be found, he would be welcome to work with the FSA in Washington. Delano's encouragement and the positive response to an exhibition of Parks's Chicago pictures at the Southside Community Center confirmed his desire to transform his feelings into visual images, to share them with the world. He was subsequently awarded the first Julius Rosenwald Fellowship in photography to work with FSA director Roy Stryker in Washington.

Stryker did not at first agree to take on the young photographer. He was afraid that racial tensions in Washington might make Parks's stay at the FSA too difficult.[9] Stryker may also have been nervous about the repercussions of adding a black photographer to the staff, since the agency was already under congressional scrutiny because of the political nature of its agenda. However, officials at the Rosenwald Foundation prevailed, and Parks moved east to join the FSA staff at the start of 1942. When he first arrived in the nation's capital in January, he encountered a city divided by race and class. He was hardly prepared for the oppression found there on the border between north and south. With a calculated understanding of the difficulties he would face, Stryker immediately proposed a series of assignments that helped Parks come to terms with racism in Washington. He began to work without a camera, looking at the voluminous picture files and writing about his experiences. His first photographs of Washington were portraits of workers on the street and children in a housing project in the city's Anacostia neighborhood. Parks soon learned that photographing intolerance "was not so easy as I assumed it would be."[10] Then Stryker suggested that he speak to Ella Watson, a government charwoman also working at the FSA. She became perhaps his most important subject.

Government charwoman, Washington, D.C., August 1942

In August 1942 Parks listened as Watson told her story. "She had struggled alone after her mother had died and her father had been killed by a lynch mob," he recalls.

> She had gone through high school, married and become pregnant. Her husband was accidentally shot to death two days before the daughter was born. By the time the daughter was eighteen she had given birth to two illegitimate children, dying two weeks after the second child's birth. What's more, the first child had been stricken with paralysis a year before its mother died. Now this woman was bringing up these grandchildren on a salary hardly suitable for one person.[11]

After hearing these words Parks asked if he could photograph her. He then exposed his first negatives of Watson, producing a series of images that today are icons of American culture. His first and best-known picture of her is *American Gothic,* 1942 (see page 33). It shows a dignified and serious woman staring straight into Parks's lens. His simple, geometric composition mimics her imperturbable stare. Looking straight into her stolid eyes, one is drawn into her world, right through any stereotypical or prototypical barriers that might normally be established by her appearance. She is posed like the farmer in Grant Wood's archetypal composition *American Gothic,* 1930, holding a broom and mop in place of the farmer's pitchfork. Behind her, hanging from above and filling the frame like a powerful, translucent beacon of irony, is the American flag. "Stryker thought it was just about the end," remembers Parks. "He said, 'My God, this can't be published, but it's a start.'"[12]

Ella Watson's gaze out of this photograph is truly transcendent. One glimpse into her eyes reveals the depth of her understanding, of the dichotomy between beauty and tragedy, and the irony implied by the limp flag hanging over her head. Clearly, a humanistic connection — a strong relationship based on some form of mutual understanding — was made between the photographer and his subject. It is apparent in this photograph that Parks, early in his career, was able to listen, understand, and silently convey his own compassion for Watson as a complex individual with a serious story to tell. It is Parks who posed Watson, who constructed the stark visual ambiguity of the scene, and whose eyes met hers at the moment the portrait was made. She looks directly at him as he stands in for the rest of us who have since encountered her stare. Here, for the first time, he was able to surpass his own feelings to express his understanding of her experience. Consequently, this photograph has become a portrait of both America and one unique individual. "Photographing bigotry was, as Stryker had warned, very difficult," wrote Parks. "The evil of its effect however, was discernible in the black faces of the oppressed and their blighted neighborhood lying within the shadows of the Capitol. It was in those shadows that the charwoman lived, and I followed her through them — to her dark house, her storefront church; to her small happinesses and daily frustrations."[13]

Parks continued to photograph Watson and her family during the ensuing months. Following on the heels of his project about poverty in Chicago's south side, her story became his second sustained photographic essay. Watson was for him symbolic of the oppression he experienced — both in Washington and in Kansas as a child — yet Parks sought to picture her life as one filled with love and spirituality as well as one fraught with difficulty. He accompanied her between work and home and photographed her environment: her apartment, street, church, and grocery store. He also depicted her adopted daughter and young grandchildren growing up in this segregated environment, creating a framework for investigating the effects of bigotry on one family and showing the various ways they had risen above them. One of the most complex and enlightening of these images is *Ella Watson and Her Grandchildren,* August 1942 (see page 34). This multilayered image cleverly unveils four generations of Watson's family together in her home. The photograph is divided into binary sections that each convey different impressions. The tension between these parts creates a meaningful narrative that begs questions about her past and the unknowable future awaiting her grandchildren.

On the left side of this picture Watson sits in her kitchen surrounded by the kids. She has just finished feeding them and everyone is relaxing, lost in thought on a hot summer evening. This domestic scene might be one from a play, framed by curtains on the left and the vertical door frame on the right. The lighting is also theatrical. As Parks looks in with his camera from outside the room, their space seems to recede illusionistically like a stage set. One sees right through to the back door and into the August twilight. The family is posed as though in a painting; Watson cradles her youngest grandchild on her lap, recalling innumerable works of art throughout history that depict a mother and child, symbols of birth and hope for the future. This is a tight-knit family group that also brings to mind the Depression-era portraits of sharecropper families by Delano, Evans, and Lee.

Religious objects and an improvised altar in the bedroom of Mrs. Ella Watson, a government charwoman, Washington, D.C., 1942

Parks's photograph is bisected vertically by the geometry of the kitchen door. While the left side portrays the family realistically — they are posed much in the spirit of 1930s documentary representation — the right side emerges like an otherworldly dream, a translucent reflection of, or counterpoint to, the theatrically constructed scene opposite. Watson's adopted daughter appears as an apparition in a hazy mirror. She is relaxed and seated, yet seems to hover within its frame. The curve created by the hem of her dress echoes the camber of the mirror as well as the lyrical calligraphy incised on the dresser under the looking glass. Like Orpheus gazing at his reflection to ponder his memories, the introspective look on the daughter's face mirrors that of Watson herself; she symbolizes a young Ella daydreaming about her future. Indeed, the daughter is smiling and looking directly at a framed photograph of an elegantly dressed couple who are, as Parks remembers, Watson's parents. They appear as a page from her family album that, after so much tragedy, emotionally connects the different people in the picture. These astutely composed links bring together each generation of the family as one, echoing Parks's portrayal of Watson as an individual with a past and a future, dreams and a harshly real present. The photograph collapses four generations of history into one complex tableau that represents both individual and collective experience.

While working at the FSA, Parks was introduced to and became particularly interested in Wright's book *12 Million Black Voices*. "In Washington during 1942 that book had become my catechism, telling me that I was at the crossroads; that voices were rising and black men were moving forward — and that I should be moving with them," wrote Parks.[14] He was referring to Wright's assertion that, "We are with the new tide. We stand at the crossroads. We watch each new procession. The hot wires carry urgent appeals. Print compels us. Voices are speaking. Men are moving! And we shall be with them."[15] Profusely illustrated with photographs by Delano, Lange, Lee, Rothstein, and Marion Post Wolcott, Wright's powerful text outlines the social legacy of slavery in America and its vast impact on African Americans. The photographs were selected and sequenced by Edwin Rosskam, a photo-editor, photographer, and writer whose efforts at the FSA also included editing and layout for Sherwood Anderson's 1940 book *Home Town*. *12 Million Black Voices* reveals Wright's panoramic sense of history, of a sweeping movement from natural to industrial culture that engages the bigotry his book decries. However, unlike his autobiographical, highly personal prose for *Black Boy* (1937), Wright's text for *12 Million Black Voices* is ubiquitous and his words speak collectively.

This book focuses on the relationship of slavery to contemporary racism and on the migration of blacks from the rural south to the urban north in order to escape poverty. Wright was, of course, telling his own story, but in speaking for all black people he couched his text in historic generalizations. "To the extent that racism was explained, it was more an economic phenomenon than a political or psychological one in *12 Million Black Voices,*" writes historian Nicholas Natanson.[16] The photographs in the book do not reveal personal stories. Most people in the pictures remain nameless, and rarely does the text refer to specific narratives found in the photographs. Through their sequencing and juxtaposition with words, the images become literal illustrations of Wright's biting prose rather than lyrical accents or symbolic counterpoint to his ideas.[17] The pictures are sometimes juxtaposed to create shocking or ironic narratives. For example, Lee's *Mother and Son, Chicago, Illinois,* and Post Wolcott's *Maid, Georgia,* are reproduced on facing pages, simultaneously revealing the living and working conditions of two black women. One is caring for her own child in a ramshackle kitchen. Another is feeding a white baby in a middle-class home.[18] Seen together, they openly compare twentieth-century servitude to nineteenth-century plantation life. "If anything, Rosskam was too single-minded in fitting — or bending — FSA pictures to the textual message," concludes Natanson.[19]

Wright's book relies on photographs to connect social concepts with nameless faces. For example, the five sections are introduced by images emblazoned with their chapter titles. One uses Delano's *Sharecropper and His Wife, Georgia,* depicting a seated black couple dressed in work clothes. Like Ella Watson in *American Gothic,* they stare straight at the viewer. The words "Inheritors of Slavery" are superimposed across the image, connecting the couple to Wright's theoretical construct and possibly to his own family, as his father had also been a sharecropper in Mississippi. Photographs of photographs were not unusual in the FSA file. In Delano's, two portraits in ornate oval frames hang on an aged wooden wall above and behind the couple's heads. They reveal a nattily dressed younger man and woman who look strikingly similar to the older couple below. As in Parks's complex work *Ella Watson and Her Grandchildren,* which also includes a framed photograph of Ella's parents, Delano collapsed time by posing the sharecropper and his wife in front of images from their family album, revealing the social effects of history on their lives. Delano's representation is personal. It tells one family's story. Alternately, Wright's words are historical, "purporting to render a broad picture of the processes of Negro life in the United States."[20] Together these words and pictures create a sequential recitation that provides, as Parks sought, "a hard look backward at black history; to realize the burdens of those who lived through it."[21] The intricate visual sequence found in *12 Million Black Voices* helped guide Parks in his search for a narrative strategy to express his own story. In Wright's book he also discovered that photographs could stand on their own, shedding their illustrative relationship to the text that Rosskam had established in the layout.

In *12 Million Black Voices* one sees that documentary pictures — images wrought from life — do not always tell the truth. In this context they reflect it, embellish it, and hammer on it. However, they do not necessarily convey the experiences of the photographers. When cropped and framed by words, or placed in carefully edited sequences, these pictures become interpretive images of the mind. They stand for a glance at history, one that constantly reinvents itself as people's lives and memories change. The fact that Wright was given a voice, and the photographs echo it without looking away, was of seminal interest for Parks, who went on to establish his own unique vision. He had also been a witness to history, and his inquiring point of view began to define events for a wide audience.

The opportunity to work with Stryker, who challenged Parks to simplify his way of seeing and to metaphorically convey the emotional substance of the topics he photographed, was pivotal in the development of Parks's mature style. It was for him a crossroads on his journey, a time and place where he had to focus his future direction. His proximity to some of the best documentary photographers in the country also helped Parks understand the complexities of visual storytelling and the fine lines drawn between truth and fiction in picturing the real world. "Despite the racial pressures, what I had learned within the year outdistanced the bigotry I encountered, and the experience had proved to be so important to my training as a documentary journalist," he wrote.[22] By 1943 the FSA was disbanded for political reasons. Stryker and some photographers, including Parks, were reassigned to the Office of War Information (OWI), where they photographed a variety of activities related to the nation's war effort. Parks traveled from New England to Florida and documented the training of black air force pilots in Michigan. He was eventually refused permission to accompany the 332nd Fighter Group to Europe, denying publicity to African American participation in the war.

Parks brought with him from the FSA to the OWI, to the Standard Oil (New Jersey) Photography Project, and ultimately to *Life* magazine, the concepts he learned of photographic truth and fiction, and of their relationship to history. At *Life,* where he worked as a staff photographer from 1948 to 1970, he found truth in his own observations and sharpened its edge to encompass his own experiences. His most important stories for *Life* include photographic essays about a Harlem gang, crime, segregation in the South, an impoverished Brazilian family, the Black Muslims, the Black Panthers, and poverty in America. He has more recently turned his observations into fictional stories and films that have been as influential as his journalistic essays. His "novel from life," *The Learning Tree* (1963), based on recollections of his childhood in Kansas, is a quasi-autobiographical narrative that relies, to varying degrees, on the vagaries of memory and the superimposition of fictional elements on a factual story. His award-winning film of the same title, completed in 1969, was a groundbreaking venture. It was one of the first Hollywood motion pictures directed by an African American filmmaker. Parks went on to make *Shaft* (1971), *Leadbelly* (1976), *Solomon Northup's Odyssey* (1984), and a number of other significant films. Since 1985 his still photographs have grown progressively abstract as he has combined his external vision with his internal feelings to create an extended series of poetic, constructed landscapes.

After gaining prominence as a photographer, Parks was able to move fluidly back and forth between various dichotomies — black and white, rich and poor, politics and entertainment, journalism and art, truth and fiction — to observe and report his feelings. Today he is recognized as a preeminent artist who has made significant contributions to the media of photography, film, literature, music, and poetry. His stories are personal, sometimes autobiographical, and they mimic his actual life. However, his greatest achievement remains that, while still young, he overcame both personal and social adversity to fulfill his potential to dream, to express the lessons of his early life, and to impart them to future generations. His breakthrough came in 1942 while photographing for the FSA. Since then he has never looked away from his past.

Photography has connected Parks to his memories, which he now stockpiles, reworks, and brings to life over and over again. He continues to find new forms with which to interpret them, moving easily between the various expressive possibilities he has mastered. His recollections, experiences, and family albums inspired his study of the truth, which forced him to make the choices he has struggled with throughout his life. This "choice of weapons," as he calls it, led him on journeys through many doors that have had an impact on numerous lives. Parks's art has now changed the way we perceive and remember chronic issues, such as race, poverty, and crime, just as it has influenced our understanding of beauty: of nature, landscape, childhood, fashion, and memory. It has changed our perceptions by soliciting an emotional response.

Two members of the St. Martin's Spiritual Church, sitting beneath the emblem of the crucifixion of Jesus on Calvary, listening to a deacon pray, Washington, D.C., 1942

NOTES

1 Tim O'Brien, *The Things They Carried* (Boston: Houghton Mifflin, 1990), p. 40.
2 Richard Wright, *Black Boy: A Record of Childhood and Youth* (New York: Harper and Brothers, 1945), p. 226.
3 Gordon Parks, *A Choice of Weapons* (St. Paul: Minnesota Historical Society Press, 1986), p. 174.
4 Ibid., p. 178.
5 Ibid.
6 Ibid., p. 273.
7 Gordon Parks, *Moments Without Proper Names* (New York: Viking, 1975), p. 7.
8 Parks, *Weapons*, p. 208.
9 Gordon Parks, interview by Philip Brookman, 22 February 1997.
10 Parks, *Weapons*, p. 230.
11 Ibid., pp. 230–231.
12 "Interview with Gordon Parks," by Richard K. Doud, Archives of American Art, Smithsonian Institution, Washington, D.C., 30 December 1964, p. 7.
13 Gordon Parks, *Voices in the Mirror: An Autobiography* (New York: Doubleday, 1990), p. 84.
14 Ibid., p. 145.
15 Richard Wright, *12 Million Black Voices* (New York: Thunder's Mouth Press, 1988), p. 147.
16 Nicholas Natanson, *The Black Image in the New Deal: The Politics of FSA Photography* (Knoxville: University of Tennessee Press, 1992), p. 246.
17 At the time the best example of such lyrical photo-text editing with FSA photographs was Archibald MacLeish, *Land of the Free* (New York: Harcourt Brace, 1938). MacLeish alternates photographs, many by Dorothea Lange, with his own poetry on opposing pages. His strategy has been praised for imbuing the photographs with greater meaning and criticized for imposing new meanings on them. See John Rogers Puckett, *Five Photo-Textual Documentaries from the Great Depression*, (Ann Arbor: UMI Research Press, 1984), pp. 45–60.
18 Wright, *12 Million*, pp. 132–133.
19 Natanson, p. 249.
20 Wright, *12 Million*, p. xix.
21 Parks, *Voices*, p. 86.
22 Ibid.

Selected Bibliography / Filmography

This selected bibliography does not include innumerable photographs and essays by Gordon Parks published in *Life* between 1948 and 1970. A record of many of his *Life* assignments, both published and unpublished, is found in *The Photographs of Gordon Parks* by Martin H. Bush, Wichita, Kans.: Wichita State University Press, 1983. A definitive bibliography is published in *An Educator's Guide to Half Past Autumn: The Art of Gordon Parks*, Washington, D.C.: Corcoran Gallery of Art, 1997.

Books, Articles, Essays, Interviews, and Films by Gordon Parks

Books

Arias in Silence. Boston: Bulfinch Press, 1994.
Born Black. Philadelphia: Lippincott, 1971.
Camera Portraits: Techniques and Principles of Documentary Portraiture. New York: F. Watts, 1948.
A Choice of Weapons. New York: Harper and Row, 1966; repr. St. Paul: Minnesota Historical Society Press, 1986.
Flash Photography. New York: Grosset and Dunlap, 1947.
Flavio. New York: W. W. Norton, 1978.
Glimpses Toward Infinity. Boston: Little, Brown, 1996.
Gordon Parks: In Love. Philadelphia: Lippincott, 1971.
Gordon Parks: A Poet and His Camera. New York: Viking Press, 1968.
Gordon Parks: Whispers of Intimate Things. New York: Viking Press, 1971.
The Learning Tree. New York: Harper and Row, 1963.
Moments Without Proper Names. New York: Viking Press, 1975.
Shannon. Boston: Little, Brown, 1981.
To Smile in Autumn. New York: W. W. Norton, 1979.
Voices in the Mirror: An Autobiography. New York: Doubleday, 1990.

Articles, Essays, and Photographs

"Brotherhood." *Crisis* 79 (October 1972): 274–275.
"Gordon Parks." *Camera* 39 (January 1960): 4–21.
"Gordon Parks: Photos (with excerpts from *A Choice of Weapons*)." *Camera* 45 (October 1966): 14–33.
Foreword. *Growing Up in New York: Photographs by Arthur Leipzig*. 1995.
Foreword. *Harlem Document: Photographs 1932–1940/Aaron Siskind* (text from Federal Writers' Project, edited by Ann Banks). Providence, R.I.: Matrix, 1981, and Washington, D.C.: Smithsonian Institution Press, 1990.
Foreword. *In the Alleys: Kids in the Shadow of the Capitol*, by Godfrey Frankel. Washington: Smithsonian Institution Press, 1995.
"A Last Visit to Leadbelly." *New York*, 10 May 1976, 66–68.
"A Matter of Conscience." *Antaeus* 49/50 (spring/summer 1983): 138–150.
Foreword. *Songs of My People: African Americans, A Self-Portrait*, by Eric Easter, Michael Cheers, and Dudley Brooks. Boston: Little, Brown, 1992.
Photographic portraits. *13 Against the Odds*, by Edward R. Embree. New York: Viking Press, 1946.
"The World of Villa Lobos: Impressions in Words and Photographs." *Show* 2 (November 1962): 76–83.

Interviews

"Beyond the Black Film: An Interview with Gordon Parks." By T. Shepard. *Cineaste* 8 (1977): 38–40.
"Gordon Parks, Director of Film *Leadbelly* and Photographer with Show at International Center of Photography." *New York Times*, 3 December 1973, 36:1.
"Gordon Parks Interview." NBC, 30 min., Library of Congress, 13 May 1977.
"Gordon Parks Interview." By Roy Campanella. *Millimeter* 4 (April 1976): 30–32.
"Gordon Parks Interview." By Maurice Peterson. *Essence* 3 (October 1972): 62.
"Gordon Parks: A Passionate Vision." *Wichita Eagle and Beacon*, 1994.
"Gordon Parks Talks About Learning Tree." By Michael Lindsay. *Cinema* 5 (1 [1969]): 14–19.
"Interview with Gordon Parks." By Richard K. Doud, Archives of American Art, Smithsonian Institution, Washington, D.C., 30 December 1964.
"*Leadbelly* Speaks for Every Black Who's Catching Hell." By Charlayne Hunter, *New York Times*, 4 July 1976, 2, 11:1.
"Purple Passage." By K. Richardson and E. Henderson. *Stills* 21 (October 1985): 12.
"A Talk with Gordon Parks." By B. Thomas. *Action* 7 (4 [July–August 1972]): 14–18.
"TV Film Looks at Slavery." By L. Bennetts. *New York Times*, 18 February 1985, C18.

Films

Flavio, 1964. 12 minutes, 16mm. Director, screenplay.
Diary of a Harlem Family, 1968. 20 minutes, 16mm. Narrator, still photographer.
The World of Piri Thomas, 1968. 60 minutes, 16mm. Director.
The Learning Tree, 1969. 107 minutes, 35mm. Director, producer, screenplay (adapted from his novel), music.
Shaft, 1971. 100 minutes, 35mm. Director.
Shaft's Big Score! 1972. 104 minutes, 35mm. Director.

The Super Cops, 1974. 94 minutes, 35mm. Director.
Leadbelly, 1976. 126 minutes, 35mm. Director.
Solomon Northup's Odyssey, 1984. 113 minutes, 16mm, made for TV. Director, screenplay.
Moments Without Proper Names, 1987. 60 minutes, 16mm. Director, screenplay, music.
Martin, 1989. 55 minutes, video. Director, script, music.

Books, Exhibition Catalogues, Articles, and Films About Gordon Parks

Books

Berry, S. L. *Gordon Parks*. New York: Chelsea House, 1991.

Bogle, Donald. *Toms, Coons, Mulattoes, Mammies and Bucks: An Interpretive History of Blacks in American Film*. New York: Viking Press, 1973, pp. 226–227.

Capa, Cornell, ed. *The Concerned Photographer*. New York: Grossman Publishers, 1972.

Chapnick, Howard. *Truth Needs No Ally*. Kansas City: University of Missouri Press, 1994.

Coleman, A. D. *Light Readings, a Photography Critic's Writings, 1968–1978*. New York: Oxford University Press, 1979.

Danska, Herbert. *Gordon Parks*. New York: T. Y. Crowell, 1971.

Dixon, Penelope, ed. *Photographers of the Farm Security Administration, 1930–1980*. Garland Reference Library of the Humanities, vol. 373. New York: Garland, 1983.

Donloe, Darlene. *Gordon Parks: Photographer, Writer, Composer, Film Maker*. Los Angeles: Melrose Square, 1993.

Fleischhauer, Carl, and Beverly W. Brannan. *Documenting America: 1935–1943*. Berkeley: University of California Press/Library of Congress, 1988.

Gaiownik, Melissa. "Parks, Gordon." In *Black Writers: A Selection of Sketches from Contemporary Authors*. Detroit: Gale Research Inc., 1989, 447–449.

Guimond, James. *American Photography and the American Dream*. Chapel Hill: University of North Carolina Press, 1991.

Harnan, Terry. *Gordon Parks: Black Photographer and Film Maker*. Champaign, Ill.: Garrard, 1972.

Hurley, F. Jack. *Portrait of a Decade*. Baton Rouge: Louisiana State University Press, 1972.

Monaco, James. "The Black Film and the Black Image." In *American Film Now*. New York: Oxford University Press, 1979, pp. 185–213.

Natanson, Nicholas. *The Black Image in the New Deal: The Politics of FSA Photography*. Knoxville: University of Tennessee Press, 1992.

Newhall, Beaumont. *The History of Photography*. New York: The Museum of Modern Art, 1949.

Palazzoli, D. *Photography: Venice '79*. New York: Rizzoli International Publications, 1979.

Powell, Richard J. *Black Art and Culture in the 20th Century*. London: Thames and Hudson, 1997.

Rothstein, Arthur, et al. *A Vision Shared: The Words and Pictures of the FSA Photographers, 1935–1943*. New York: St. Martin's Press, 1976.

Scherman, David E., ed. *The Best of Life*. New York: Time-Life Books, 1973.

Shepard, Thomas. "Gordon Parks: Beyond the Black Film." In *Cineaste Interviews: On the Art and Politics of the Cinema*. Edited by Dan Georgakas and Lenny Rubenstein. Chicago: Lake View Press, 1983, pp. 173–180.

Stange, Maren. *Symbols of Ideal Life: Social Documentary Photography in America, 1890–1950*. Cambridge: Cambridge University Press, 1989.

Stryker, Roy E., and Nancy Wood. *In this Proud Land: America, 1935–1943*. Boston: New York Graphic Society, 1973.

Trachtenberg, Alan. *Reading American Photographs: Images as History — Mathew Brady to Walker Evans*. New York: Hill and Wang, 1989.

Turk, Midge. *Gordon Parks*. New York: Crowell, 1971.

Tidyman, Ernest. *Shaft*. New York: Macmillan, 1970.

Willis, Deborah, and Jane Lusaka, eds. *Visual Journal: Harlem and D.C. in the Thirties and Forties*. Washington, D.C.: The Center for African American History and Culture and Smithsonian Institution Press, 1996.

Exhibition Catalogues

Eye Music: New Images by Gordon Parks. Exhibition Catalogue. New York: Alex Rosenberg Gallery, 1979.

Gordon Parks: Photographs at Large. Exhibition Catalogue. Miami: Wolfson Gallery, Miami Dade Community College, 1981.

The Gordon Parks Collection: Kansas State University. Collection catalog. By Charles Stroh. Manhattan, Kans.: Kansas State University Department of Art, 1983.

The Photograph As a Permanent Color Print. Exhibition Catalogue. New York: New York Cultural Center/Fairleigh Dickinson University, 1970.

The Photographs of Gordon Parks. Exhibition Catalogue. By Martin H. Bush. Wichita, Kans.: Wichita State University Press, 1983.

Roy Stryker: U.S.A., 1943–1950, The Standard Oil (New Jersey) Photography Project. Exhibition Catalogue. By Steven W. Plattner. International Center of Photography, New York. Austin: University of Texas Press, 1983.

40 Jahre Fotografie. Exhibition Catalogue. By Thomas Buchsteiner and Karl Steinorth. Tubingen: Kodak Aktiengesellschaft in Zusammenarbeit mit dem Deutsch-Amerikanischen Institut Tubingen, 1989.

Articles

Alexander, Michael. "Gordon Parks: 'I Was Determined to Succeed.'" *Long Island Newsday Magazine*, 2 May 1976.

Alex Rosenberg Gallery. Exhi. Rev. *ArtNews* 78 (December 1979): 155.

Ames, K. "Black Legend." *Newsweek,* 6 April 1976, 95.
"Armed with a Camera." Review of *A Choice of Weapons. Time,* 18 February 1966.
Arnold, Gary. "Film: Family *'Tree.'*" *Washington Post,* 27 September 1969, C8.
"Autobiography Reviewed." *New York Times,* 13 February 1966, 7, 26.
Bosworth, Patricia. "'How Could I Forget What I Am?'" *New York Times,* 17 August 1969.
Brierly, Dean. "Renaissance Man: The Photography of Gordon Parks." *Camera and Darkroom* 13 (12 [1 December 1991]): 24.
Bunzel, Peter D. "I'm a Writer Who Happens to Be Black." *Los Angeles Herald Examiner,* 8 October 1981.
Burns, Ben. "Creative Wizardry of Gordon Parks." *Sepia* 25 (April 1976): 36–40, 44, 46.
Canaday, John. "A WASP's Progress: Growing Up White and Male in Ft. Scott, KS." *New York Times,* 19 March 1972, 6, 32.
Canby, Vincent. "The Screen: Parks's Elegiacal *Leadbelly.*" *New York Times,* 29 May 1976.
Canby, Vincent. *"Shaft."* Review. *New York Times,* 11 July 1971, 2, 1.
Clarity, James F. "Gordon Parks." *New York Times,* 9 June 1973.
Cocks, J. "*Leadbelly.*" *Time,* 24 May 1976, 76.
Coleman, A. D. "Gordon Parks: *Arias in Silence.*" *Camera and Darkroom* 17 (7 [July 1995]): 22–28.
Coleman, A. D. "Soulscapes by Gordon Parks." *American Visions* 8 (1 [February 1993]): 14–19.
Daugherty, Greg. "Flavio: A Famous Photo Essay Revisited." *Professional Photographer* (April 1978).
Dempsey, David. "Witness to a Killing." Review of *The Learning Tree. New York Times,* 15 September 1963.
DiGrappa, Carol. "Inner Visions." *Camera Arts* (March–April 1982).
Dyson, Eric. Review of *Voices in the Mirror. New York Times,* 9 December 1990, 7, 19:1.
Ebert, Roger. "A Black Pioneer Behind the Camera." *Chicago Sun-Times,* 2 July 1972.
Ferdinand, Val. Review of *Whispers of Intimate Things. Black World* 22 (August 1973): 80–86.
Fitzgerald, Sheryl. "Gordon Parks: Picturing Beauty." *New York Times,* 2 March 1980.
Ford, Colin. "Gordon Parks: An Artist Reminisces." *New York Times,* 3 December 1975.
Fowler, Giles M. "With Camera and Script, Parks Goes Home Again." *Kansas City Star,* 6 October 1968, 1D–2D.
Glueck, Grace. "Gordon Parks at Alex Rosenberg Gallery." Exh. Rev. *New York Times,* 26 October 1979, 3, 20:6.
"Gordon Parks." *Camera* 45 (October 1966): 14–33.
"Gordon Parks' Photographs." *U.S. Camera* 6 (no. 9 [December 1943]): 16–19.
Gould, Jack. "Portrait of Gordon Parks." *New York Times,* 24 April 1968.
Greenspun, Roger. "Screen: Saul Gumshoe." Review of *Shaft. New York Times,* 3 July 1971, 20:1.
Grimes, William. "Parks's Works to Go to Library of Congress." *New York Times,* 7 July 1995.
Grumbach, Doris. Review of *Flavio. New York Times,* 26 March 1978, 7, 14.
Grundberg, Andy. "Gordon Parks at the New York Public Library." Exh. Rev. *New York Times,* 1 March 1987, 2, 35:1.
Grundberg, Andy. "Living a Life of Talent in a Land of Prejudice." Review of *Voices in the Mirror. New York Times,* 8 January 1991, C15:1.
Hamill, Dennis. "The Sum of His Art, Gordon Parks." *New York Daily News,* 26 January 1997.
Hewitt, Mary Jane. "The Eye Music of Gordon Parks." *International Review of African American Art,* 8 (4 [1989]): 50–63.
Higgins, Chester A., Sr. *"To Smile in Autumn."* Review. *Crisis,* 8 July 1981, 296.
Jennings, Robert C. "Under the Learning Tree." *Los Angeles Times Magazine,* 19 October 1969.
Koelln, Georgann. "Gordon Parks." *St. Paul Dispatch,* 21 April 1980.
Kramer, Hilton. "Art: Empathy of Gordon Parks." *New York Times,* 4 October 1975, 19:1.
Lauerman, Connie. "Author Gordon Parks: At 68, the Best Is Yet to Come." *Chicago Tribune,* 21 September 1981.
Moore, Deedee. "Martin." *American Visions,* 1 December 1989, 34.
Moore, Deedee. "Is There Anything Gordon Parks Can't Do?" *Smithsonian,* 1 April 1989, 66.
Myers, Walter Dean. "Gordon Parks: John Henry with a Camera." *Black Scholar* 7 (January–February 1976): 26–30.
Perry, Jean. "The Universal Man." *New York Daily News,* 3 October 1977.
Pugh, Donna. "Gordon and Cleo: Two Artists in Collaboration." *Dance News* (May 1979).
Raynor, Vivien. "Gordon Parks' *Moments Without Proper Names* at White Plains, N.Y., Public Library." Exh. Rev. *New York Times,* 26 January 1992, 12, 15:1.
Redding, Saunders. "In America." Review of *A Choice of Weapons. New York Times,* 3 February 1966.
Reed, Rex. "Movies." Review of *Leadbelly. Vogue* 166 (January 1976): 33.
Simpson, Coreen. "Masters of Photography." *The Black American* (February 1980).
Smith, Caroline. "Cover Story." *British Journal of Photography* 140. (6945 [21 October 1994]): 10.
Snedaker, Kit. "Renaissance Man." *Los Angeles Herald Examiner,* 28 September 1969.
Terry, Wallace. "He Refuses to Limit Himself." *Parade Magazine,* 21 July 1996, 4–5.
Trescott, Jacqueline. "Images of a Master Observer." *Washington Post,* 20 October 1978.
"Who, What, When, Where, Why: Show on Gordon Parks." *New York Times,* 24 April 1968, 95:4.
Wilson, Judith. "*To Smile in Autumn.*" Review. *Essence* 11 (June 1980): 21.

Films

Forma, Warren, and Gordon Parks. *The Weapons of Gordon Parks.* 1970.
Kuralt, Charles. "A Look at the Works of Gordon Parks." *Sunday Morning,* CBS, 1982.
Sills, Beverly. "Can One Man Live Six Lives?" *Skyline Show,* PBS, 1980.

List of Plates

The portfolio sections of this book do not follow the conventional chronology of a retrospective but were creatively arranged by Gordon Parks like a musical composition — the visual equivalent of a tone poem.

Acknowledgments

I HOLD HIGH PRAISE for one who, more than any other, helped pull this book together — Johanna Fiore, my devoted friend and indefatigable assistant. She stood firm against odds that assaulted my mind and body during the ordeal. When I was feeling like a stone, she pushed me through days so tiring, fatigue held them nameless. Photographs, many unseen for years, became her prey and burden. Her searching, sorting, and packaging went on for months. When time seemed to have lost its senses, her voice pierced the haze. "Well, we made a lot of progress today." I listened without hearing. Too many stacks of bulging envelopes frowned at me. Finally, having dealt with my ordeal until I was whole again, Johanna had done what she set out to do. I'm grateful for having her at my side, and I don't know how or when I will repay her. Just recently the camera has also set fire to her imagination. Since I live so close to the center of this new flame, I hope to keep it burning.

Gently guiding me through the smoke of all the bonfires was my steadfast editor, Terry Reece Hackford. We met as strangers, like two people sentenced to walk in the same shoe. In such a pinched situation, an amicable walk can be difficult. But soon we were moving as one. That shoe belonged to both of us, and I feel immeasurably rich for having shared it with Terry — a superb editor and a fine human being.

Philip Brookman, Curator of Photography and Media Arts at the Corcoran Gallery of Art, lent sage advice during his visits to my home in New York. For the book and my exhibition, he always brought order to something in need of order. My faith in him grew steadily from the beginning, and that faith remains unbroken.

Eric Baker, the book's designer, was chosen because excellence is his trademark. His offering speaks nobly for itself. He lives up to his reputation, and I am grateful to him and to his talented and conscientious assistant David Blankenship for their untiring efforts on my behalf.

At times, I wandered into the darkness of *Life*'s laboratories to greet my favorite printmaker, Heike Hinsch. She was always there, like a moon in the dark, and working with the patience of a stone. Her quest for perfection never crumpled. So to Heike, my gratitude for your fidelity — and for growing weary along with me.

I could go on mentioning many people who deserve my thanks, but it would take another book to do that. They know and I know who they are, and I long to express my indebtness to each of them on these pages. But the lack of space places this longing beyond the realm of possibility. To each of them I offer a huge silent thanks — for the friendship and encouragement that helped me to know the well-being of yet another autumn.

GORDON PARKS